PROCESSMIND

PROCESSMIND

A USER'S GUIDE TO CONNECTING WITH THE MIND OF GOD

ARNOLD MINDELL, PH.D.

QUEST

BOOKS

Theosophical Publishing House
Wheaton, Illinois • Chennai, India

Quest Books
Theosophical Publishing House
P. O. Box 270
Wheaton, IL 60187-0270

www.questbooks.net

Cover design by Dan Doolin

Library of Congress Cataloging-in-Publication Data

Mindell, Arnold.
Processmind: A User's Guide to Connecting with the Mind of God / Arnold Mindell.
    p.   cm.
Includes bibliographical references and index.
ISBN 978-0-8356-0886-2
1. Consciousness. 2. Mind and body. 3. Spirit. I. Title. II. Title: Processmind.

BF311.M5535 2010
153—dc22   2010015653

5   4   3   2   *   11   12   13   14

Printed in the United States of America

CONTENTS

CONTENTS

ILLUSTRATIONS

Acknowledgments

Amy Mindell, my best friend, partner, and colleague, helped me with every inch of this book, experiencing, experimenting, and testing processmind details. I am eternally grateful to her for her awesome collaboration and presence at every imaginable level.

I am indebted to Susan Kocen once again for her creative labor in writing up the recordings of lectures and seminars that formed the basis for this book.

To all my colleagues and students around the world, thank you, friends, for having tested this book thousands of times.

Thanks to Max Schupbach and Joe Goodbread for many clarifying conversations. I am grateful to Dawn Menken and Robert King, who contributed greatly to improving the original manuscript with their many insightful and helpful comments.

I am indebted to the Deep Democracy Institute and the Process Work Institutes around the world for their interest and assistance with the many details of this work.

And once again, I want to especially thank Ms. Margaret Ryan for her sense of humor, friendship, and editing expertise! Ms. Charlene Sieg was also helpful with the final copy.

The people at Quest have been wonderful in their understanding, commitment to, and appreciation of this book. Thanks, Richard Smoley, for your enthusiasm. Thank you, Sharron Dorr, for managing the creation of *Processmind*, and thank you, Carolyn Bond, for your skillful editing help.

And thanks to Albert Einstein for his comment: "I want to know God's thoughts . . . the rest are details."

INTRODUCTION

This book is my response to Einstein's famous wish: "I want to know God's thoughts . . . the rest are details." Most likely, no human being can ever truly know "God's thoughts"—that is, the mind of God. Rather, our task is to consistently ask, "What *is* the mind of God?" That question is inherent in every sentence of this book.

Early in my career, I studied science because I wanted to understand the mind of nature. Eventually I realized that to understand the mind of nature, I also had to understand the observer's role as a participant in the laws of nature—I had to study psychology. My work in psychology evolved into forty-five years of experience working with individuals and large groups of people in all states of consciousness.

Throughout my career I have been confronted daily with the presence of the laws of nature as they operate behind all human and environmental processes.

These laws originate in "God's mind," so to speak. Thus all life processes have their roots in that mind also. This mind as it is present in some way behind all life processes I call the *processmind*. The processmind is the palpable, intelligent, organizing "force field" present behind our personal and large group processes and, like other deep quantum patterns, behind processes of the universe. *Processmind* is an attempt to extend and deepen our quest to know this field and these patterns as they are understood today in physics by connecting them to experiences studied and recorded in psychology and mysticism.

In this book I not only explore the many aspects of the processmind; I also show how it can help us to alleviate the pain of symptoms, facilitate relationships, and reconfigure organizational problems in a wide range of global and everyday situations.

In this exploration, *you*, dear reader, are the goal. By guiding you into your processmind, I intend this book to be one of your trainings. Though I am excited by processmind ideas and want to convince you of their usefulness by references to physics, psychology, mythology, and spiritual traditions, my central goal is not intellectual. Rather, it is to encourage you to try out these new methods on issues of all sorts. The processmind's existence will probably seem reasonable after studying its appearance in science and religion. However, for me, the final test is that most people can train themselves to use it to resolve both personal and world problems.

This book is divided into four parts. Part one examines in detail how the processmind is present as the deepest part of yourself. Once you have learned more about the processmind, the rest of the book encourages you to use it as a tool to enhance your life skills and belief system. Part two focuses on how accessing the processmind can help resolve body and relationship issues and reverse the downward turn of global problems. Part three explores the processmind's link to your highest principles and to the states of consciousness implied by spiritual systems. Part four takes a deeper look at the physics and psychology of nonlocality and how the processmind "self-organizes" relationship energies and can potentially contribute to positive world change.

The conclusion connects processmind ideas to ancient African community ethics and to Gandhi's principle of *ahimsa* (nonviolence) and shows how the processmind updates and explains these ethics. The glossary offers definitions of key terms used in physics and in process oriented psychology. Appendix A considers the relationship between the quantum mind—a concept discussed in some of my earlier books—and this new concept of processmind.

Starting with chapter 2, each chapter offers exercises that enrich your awareness of the processmind as discussed in that chapter. I suggest you do these exercises. Appendix B, the Processmind Collage, provides page space designated by chapter where you can log the processmind experiences that occur while you do the exercises. Keeping track this way of your experiences can tell you a lot about who you are and can be helpful in dealing with real-world situations.

This book is a kind of user's guide to everyday life and to the universe's hidden dimensions. At the same time, I advise against simply believing any processmind theory or related belief system about the universe's possible code, even this one. Don't believe anything until you test and prove that it works in your own life. Such a stance of healthy doubt will, I hope, bring the spiritual traditions and sciences closer together.

PART ONE

THE PROCESSMIND IN YOUR PERSONAL LIFE

Figure 0.1. Albert Einstein.

CHAPTER 1

PROCESSMIND AS A FORCE FIELD IN EVERYDAY LIFE AND NEAR DEATH

Just about everyone wonders now and then if there is some kind of intelligence organizing the apparently random and creative events in personal life and the universe. Are those events haphazard . . . or is some kind of "mind" at work in the background? How might our awareness of such events influence them?

In my practice, I have often wondered about the mysterious power that seems to appear throughout life, especially in moments of crisis and near death. What is this power that not only produces the most amazing and helpful experiences but is also behind our ongoing difficulties and conflicts, our environmental problems . . . *and* our ability to make peaceful changes? Science and spiritual traditions both contribute answers. Yet in the twenty-first century, we are far from a consensus about what or who we are, and what, if anything, arranges or "co-creates" our fate.

Modern leading scientists such as Albert Einstein as well as ancient world spiritual traditions have believed there is an intelligent cosmic force behind it all. Yet Einstein doubted that science had found it. In a 1926 letter to his colleague Max Born, he made a remark now well-known among theoretical physicists: "Quantum mechanics is certainly imposing. But an inner voice tells me it is not yet the real thing. The theory says a lot, but does not really bring us any closer to the secret of the Old One."[1]

3

Today, about a century after the discoveries of quantum theory and relativity, cosmologists are still wondering about "the secret of the Old One." Stephen Hawking and Paul Davies refer to the intelligent force Einstein sought as the "mind of God."[2] Some theoretical physicists hope to find this "mind" in unified field theories or related concepts. C. G. Jung, Roberto Assagioli, and other depth psychologists speak of a "collective unconscious," the "transpersonal Self," or some type of transcendent or "unitive" consciousness. Quoting sixteenth-century alchemists, Jung and his friend Wolfgang Pauli, a Nobel prize-winning quantum physicist, speculated about unified psychophysical region of experience—the "Unus Mundus." Religions have always spoken of the design, powers, and wisdom of the universe in terms of a Self, a God, or gods.

I call Einstein's "Old One" the *processmind*. By *processmind* I mean an organizing factor—perhaps *the* organizing factor—that operates both in our personal lives and in the universe. Studying and experiencing this processmind will connect the now separate disciplines of psychology, sociology, physics, and mysticism and provide new useful ways to relate to one another and the environment. The processmind is both inside of you and, at the same time, apparently connected to everything you notice. I will show that your processmind is in your brain yet is also "nonlocal," allowing you to be in several places at the same time.

When I first began writing, I was afraid that this nonlocal nature of the processmind, foreshadowed in quantum physics, might sound too strange. But then I realized that at least some people sense nonlocality every morning in those hypnagogic states just between sleeping and waking. In this "half sleep–half awake" state a kind of dreamlike intelligence frequently gives us "nonlocal" information about people and things in distant places. A physicist might call this experience the psychological counterpart of "quantum entanglement" (which I explain in a later chapter). Today I realize that the processmind is not just a specific altered state of consciousness; it defines the lifestyle and political view we need to resolve the deepest outer as well as inner conflicts.

In any case, the processmind can be experienced as a kind of force field. It is an active, intelligent "space" between the observer and observed. It is both you and me and the "us" we share. It is connected to the facts of everyday reality but also independent of them. After much exploring, both in myself and in people near death, I think it likely that the processmind has qualities that extend beyond our present concepts of life and death.

QUANTUM MIND AND PROCESSMIND

The concept of the processmind expands upon all my earlier work, especially the book *Quantum Mind*, which I wrote about ten years ago. The quantum mind is that aspect of our psychology that corresponds to basic aspects of quantum physics. The quantum aspect of our awareness notices the tiniest, easily overlooked "nano" tendencies and self-reflects upon these subliminal experiences. However, the quantum mind is not just a supersensitive self-reflecting awareness; it also is a kind of "pilot wave" or guiding pattern. In *Quantum Mind*, I suggested that the math (Schrödinger's wave equation) and rules of quantum physics mirror our ability to self-reflect and to create everyday reality. Physicists speak of the wave function "collapsing" to create reality. I speak about how our self-reflection uses and then marginalizes, rather than "collapses," our dreaming nature. For example, after reflecting on a dream, you might think, "Ah ha! Now I will do this or that"; then you put the dreamworld aside temporarily while you take action in order to create a new reality.

Besides the ability we share with other parts of our universe to sense possibilities, self-reflect, and move from dreaming to everyday reality, we may have the ability to be in two places or two states at the same time, just as quantum physics suggests that material particles can behave. For example, in a dream you may be at once dead and alive—even though upon awakening, you come out of this unitive experience and soon begin reflecting, identifying with one or another of the dream images. Thus, we can characterize our quantum nature as nonlocal or "bilocal" as well as highly sensitive and self-reflective.

The processmind expands upon these characteristics of the quantum mind by adding one more crucial quality: Our deepest self, our processmind, is not just sensitive, self-reflective, and "bilocal"; it can also be found in mystical traditions. In particular, it can be sensed in terms of what Aboriginal peoples have identified as an individual's or group's "totem spirit." Our processminds are related, not just to general physical characteristics of the quantum universe, but to particular earth-based characteristics experienced as, or associated with, what shamans have called "power spots"—special places on earth that we love and trust. The processmind is a force field that has been identified with "totem spirits," that is, with subtle feelings we have about places on earth that tend to "move" us into feeling wise and/or in particular directions.

What are these totem spirits and earth feelings? This is like asking what is under a rock without moving the rock and actually looking beneath it. Presently, our main method of "looking" is our own process of awareness. At first, the natural scientist in me stopped here and said: "Hey! Wait a minute! Earth-based totem spirits or power spots manifesting our processminds? Don't believe it! Your mind is in your brain, and your brain is in your head!"

But then the therapist in me says, "Of course your mind is partly in your brain. But your brain is matter, and matter has nonlocal characteristics. It's just possible that some of these characteristics are—at the very least—projected upon the earth's power spots. Aboriginal people have always felt that special earth spots, such as burial grounds, are power areas and have identified with them. So, dear scientific skeptic, in the experiments that follow please remain skeptical yet open-minded enough to use the results to explore the mind's possible nonlocality on the basis of your own experience. In doing so, perhaps you will eventually sense and remember that part of your evolutionary psychology that once knew how to follow the earth and its associated powers. Most people normally identify themselves as a body at a particular location. But in deep sleep and near death, when your ordinary self is less prominent, your whole, *nonlocalized* mind—that is, your processmind—becomes more apparent. This powerful organizing factor appears as if it were a kind of "force field," like the wind that blows through the trees. Normally you can't see force fields, you can only feel and notice how they move things around——as the wind moves the leaves. Just as shamans of indigenous cultures refer to the figures personifying these invisible fields as "allies" or "guides," physicists refer to the structures of fields such as electromagnetism as field equations mediated by "virtual particles." Whether we call them *allies, equations,* or *particles,* all such dynamics can give us a sense of the power and structure of invisible fields.

Probably our most common experience of an invisible force field is with that of gravity. You can feel the force of gravity on your body just by jumping up into the air and inevitably being pulled back down to earth. (On the moon, you would take longer to come back down because the field of gravity is weaker there than on earth.)

But even though the force of gravity organizes all of our motions, because we are so used to existing in its field, we rarely think of it. In the same way, we rarely pay attention to the psychophysical force field of processmind unless we are in a sensitive or altered state of consciousness, dreaming, or near death. Nevertheless, the processmind, like gravity, organizes great portions of our lives.

Let me briefly summarize what I have said until now. What I call the *processmind*—as it appears in quantum physics and to which Einstein refers as the "Old One"—is the imagined intelligence behind the laws of the individual and the universe. Depending upon the context, I use the word *processmind* to mean:

- A theory; an organizing principle in psychology and physics
- A field concept and experience of being moved by a specific altered state of consciousness
- A practice; a meditation and mediation procedure found in the exercises of this book

- The deepest self; a somatic experience of wellness and least action
- A nondualistic quality that describes a particular quantum-like, human awareness system
- A belief in the spirits or gods found in religions or spiritual traditions
- A life or near-death experience that includes all of the foregoing

SARA'S LAST VERBAL COMMUNICATION

I was reminded of the processmind field recently when a friend and colleague of mine, Dr. Sara Halprin, a therapist and author, became ill and shortly thereafter died. From her earliest childhood, Sara had been interested in theater and writing, in portraying things to the public. In many ways, she is, or was, a grand woman. When she became ill, and with the help of her partner, Dr. Herb Long, I was fortunately able to speak with her several times over the phone, though we were in different cities. It turns out that the words I shall now relate, which occurred while Sara and I last spoke, were in her last shared verbal experience. (Thanks to my partner, Amy, for having recorded them.) I had no idea that this would be Sara's final conversation or that she would die within days. In retrospect, she may have been suffering in part from an extra large dose of chemotherapy, which her body was not tolerating very well.

As that last conversation began, Sara told me in a weak but clear voice that, above all, she wanted her life to be useful to others. She spoke of her recent attempts to find the best available doctors, hospitals, and medicine to help her with her kidney cancer and asked if I knew of anything that could be done above and beyond the types of medicine and chemotherapy she was already trying. I told her that she was getting the best medical help I knew of and that the most helpful thing to do was to follow her process. She agreed.

As we talked, she shared that she was very anxious. She complained of panic, of a rapid heart beat and dreadful fear. Breathing very quickly, she asked several times, "What is happening?" Perhaps she was afraid because she sensed how close she was to death. The following is an almost verbatim report of her experiences:

She said her heart was "racing," beating so violently she could feel it thump in her chest. When I suggested we start with that heart experience, she became quieter. After a moment, she said in a very low and quiet voice that she saw herself "falling into nothingness . . . falling into nothingness." So I said, "Let's explore that nothingness." She said that she was afraid of falling into that nothingness: "It's so empty." I gently recommended that she trust and follow her experience. "Maybe it will turn out to be just nothing," she dismally responded.

Nevertheless, and though hesitant, Sara soon told me that she would try to explore the falling feeling. With Herb holding the phone to her ear, she reported that she saw herself spinning through the air in "emptiness." In an anxious but excited state, she said, "I'm falling, falling, falling." Frightened, she asked, "What next?" I said we should wait and her process would tell us what would be next, if anything. We waited quietly for a moment and then she said joyously, to her own (and my) surprise, that she was "landing near the river."

"I am landing, yes! I am landing on the river and am so happy to see a beautiful green mallard on the water!" She said that the bird's neck amazed her—it was "fluttering," moving rapidly back and forth. Perhaps it was about to take off. "Beautiful." After a moment of quietness, she said, "good-bye." That was her last spoken word.

Today, in retrospect, I wonder about Sara's last moments of life. I appreciate the way Herb cared for her, and I wonder about her vision. I want to wonder more with you, dear reader, and I want to thank Sara for having given me the impulse to publish her words. I remember her desire to be "useful" to others; perhaps the process she went through with me will be useful to others as well. After completing this book, I came across an autobiographical sketch in which she describes herself as a bird living by a river.[3] How remarkable that during the last months of her life she moved to a new home on the banks of the Willamette River in Portland.

Figure 1.1. Sara Halprin's Life Process.
She moved through nothingness to the mallard
on the Willamette River close to her home.

Her last verbally communicated process brings up all sorts of questions. What kind of intelligence guided her through that "emptiness" to the river and the bird? What is the nature of that intelligence within her that appeared at first in her fluttering heart and later in the mallard's? Was that terrifying heartbeat a body effect appearing because of the coming of death? Or was it her dreaming experience of the "fluttering bird"? What organizes body experiences to mirror our fantasies and dreams, or our dreams to mirror our body experiences? And what was the meaning of that "nothingness" that she feared and finally journeyed through before discovering the duck? Significantly, it was only when she finally submitted to that nothingness that her ordinary form disappeared and she focused on the bird.

Perhaps the nothingness Sara feared was death. But my guess is that what she experienced as nothingness was actually the power field of her processmind, whose organization she did not yet quite know. Once the processmind pulled her in and moved her from one form to another, her fear was replaced by amazement and quietude at her vision. Why did this field not speak to her about her death, or her burial, or the people around her? Why did it lead her instead to the bird at the riverside?

Each of us will have our own answers to these questions. Mine is that her processmind—that is, the deep intelligence moving her from one point to the next in her existence—is a timeless power field appearing in symbols, first as "emptiness" but then as a fluttering mallard on a river. It seems to me that while terms such as *life* and *death* may help us define reality, or rather "consensus reality," they are not the only, or the best, descriptions of our journey through time. The panic-stricken heart that frightened Sara the most as a symptom of impending death in the next moment became the wonderful and consoling image of a fluttering bird about to fly.

Sara's life is captured in part by a photograph of her and by images representing her final experiences in life (see figure 1.1). But she cannot be summed up in images. We are all more than the sum of our personal and imaginary pictures, in all of our realities and dreams. Sara's processmind, like ours, is a kind of emptiness, a potential, an invisible field like gravity or the wind. It is always there, pulling us, moving us, one way or another. In everyday life our ordinary minds deny the processmind in the background. We fear that emptiness—its power and its ability to move us freely and wisely in ways we see in our dreams.

SPACE AND TIME, LIFE AND DEATH

Is it not remarkable that even in Sara's last experiences, her process-mind does not speak of death? Normally, we are so concerned about life and death. However, near death the processmind seems to ignore the dimensions of time and space in order to point to another space, a "hyperspace," beyond our ordinary dimensions of day and night, future and past, you and me, life and death. In a way, thinking of our lives as a three-part sequence in which we are born, we live, and we die amounts to a marginalization of the powerful and unitive field experience that organizes the symbols of our dreams. Thinking of ourselves as either alive or dead, awake or asleep, or in terms of temporary states or appearances, or failures and successes, negates a big part of our nature.

From the viewpoint of the processmind, we are a whole field that encompasses *all* the apparent dichotomies. We are not just the images; we are the powers and presences that *create* the images and sometimes emerge into symbols such as the bird.

If this sounds strange, remember that our ancestors and Aboriginal peoples everywhere felt "fields" and personified the powers of those fields as totem spirits and certain areas of the earth, believing that we ourselves are manifestations of those spirits and areas. From this perspective, Sara was perhaps not just the woman we knew by her picture but also the power behind the images of water and bird. We need to be open to this possibility in order to appreciate and make sense of near-death experiences.

PHYSICS AND PSYCHOLOGY

In *Quantum Mind*, I agreed with physicist David Bohm that there is something like a "pilot" wave in nature. Bohm imagined his pilot wave to guide particles. It seems to me that the processmind field is what guides us through life. We need to develop a more complete picture of existence that describes both the origin of our awareness as well as our everyday reality. We need the concept of something like the processmind that includes and also extends our everyday concepts of life and death, time and space, reality and dreams.

Later I argue that the processmind is a superposition of several states, meaning that it is the sum of all our potential dream images as well as of our various everyday moods and abilities. Like Schrödinger's quantum cat who confused Schrödinger and others in its ability to be both dead and alive at the same time, our processminds are both alive and dead and more—all at the same time. Though this dual-state view may confuse our doubting, everyday minds, for which ordinary life is the only reality, it may literally be a matter of life and death (or at least a health-and-wellness issue) for our bodies to develop an expanded awareness that includes the field of our processminds. Our everyday self will always be important. We need it to help us doubt, wonder, and reflect. But it is only part of the story; it is not the whole of it. Instead, the invisible "empty" field of the processmind is what may help us understand the full dimension of life and what happens near death.

I like Suzuki Roshi's Zen metaphors for "empty mind." He says in his wonderful *Zen Mind, Beginner's Mind*: "It is necessary to believe in this nothing—voidness. But I don't mean Voidness. It is something. But that something is something that is always prepared for taking a particular form. It has rules, it has theory, or truth, in its activity." He claims, "By enlightenment, I mean believing in this nothing. Believing in something which has no form or color but is ready to take form or color."[4]

The Roshi's "nothing" is what I call the field of the processmind.

THINGS TO THINK ABOUT

1. The processmind is an update of Einstein's "mind of God" and "quantum mind" concepts.
2. The processmind is an invisible force field that moves and organizes our bodies and dream images in meaningful ways.

3. Perhaps the processmind field organizes our personal lives in both normal and unusual states of consciousness, even at the edge between life and death.
4. Doubt is important; it helps us self-reflect.
5. Empty mind in the Zen traditions, field thinking in physics, and processmind in psychology are related and, in part, overlapping concepts.

FIELDS, LIGHTNING, AND ENLIGHTENMENT

Instead of gathering knowledge, you should clear your mind. . . . This is called emptiness, or omnipotent self, or knowing everything. When you know everything, you are like a dark sky. Sometimes a flashing will come through the dark sky. After it passes, you forget all about it, and there is nothing left but the dark sky. The sky is never surprised when all of a sudden a thunderbolt breaks through. . . . When we have emptiness we are always prepared for watching the flashing.

—Shunryu Suzuki Roshi, *Zen Mind, Beginner's Mind*

In everyday, or "consensus" reality, you are simply a real body, a material, biological being that exists in a given location and time. You have weight, occupy space, and age over time. If you don't believe that, the Internal Revenue Service will remind you when it's time to pay taxes. In consensus reality you are a person living in your body. At the same time, from another viewpoint you are an invisible, nonlocal field that appears in part as the motions of a real body with real things around it.

I learned a lot about this nonlocal field by working with people in comatose and near-death situations. If, for example, I assume that a person in a comatose state is present only in his or her body in a given hospital bed, then the only responses I will notice from that person are minimal body cues. However, if I do not associate the person only with that body, then I am free to seek his or her responses anywhere I notice them in the room.

This, of course, is true of anyone with whom you communicate. We frequently experience nonlocal connection with another person. You think of someone just before he or she calls or emails, and you intuit something and see it show up in consensus reality shortly thereafter. This kind of interconnection with someone in the comatose state seems more remarkable only because we tend to minimize it in everyday experience.

I have often said to someone in a coma, "Make a sound if you hear me." If the body lying in the bed does not move but the curtain hanging in the hospital window suddenly wafts open, I might say, "Ah ha! Thanks for answering." Though I have not collected statistical evidence to demonstrate the value of this approach, in the situations in which I have worked, exploring nonlocal reactions from someone has enabled amazing body awakenings. In my book *Coma: Key to Awakening*, I report the details of one such case in which the person, after recovering from the coma, confirmed that he had heard and then "spoken" to me.

Similarly, if you identify someone who is ill or dying only with their body, you may inhibit them from telling you their experience. Why? Because who they are as a totality is marginalized. You are viewing them only as ill or dying, instead of as a whole person. For the same reason, very old people may hesitate to talk about death and dying partly because they fear that others will lock them into the idea of one locality, their failing body. This reminds me of an experience I had with my own mother in her last days. I was following her process as she lay in a vegetative state. Evidently she was actually in a remote state of consciousness, since she awakened for a moment to ask if I could "see the birth of a star in the dark space of the universe" and added, "Isn't it wonderful!"

My point is that humans are more than physical bodies; they are also processmind fields, and being aware of this fact shifts our ability to work with their processes. When needed, remember to consider yourself not only a mechanical, local body influenced by forces in the immediate vicinity but also a processmind field—an intelligence that can be anywhere anytime—manifesting as a physical body or actions around the body. Sensing your processmind is like sensing a presence, a potential, or a tendency. In this chapter we shall learn about how to be closer to that potential.

THE FIELD OF LIGHTNING

Metaphors such as the gravity field, the air pressure field creating the wind, and the electromagnetic field preceding a lightning strike can help us grasp the processmind because at its essential level it is invisible.[1] Likewise, an invisible electric field fills the space between the sky and the earth, and we can see it only in the form of lightning streaking across the sky.

Let's consider the lightning analogy. Pictures of lightning taken with a high-speed camera show how it occurs over time. The entire process illustrated in figure 2.1 takes place in one-fifth of a second. Frame 1 shows the electric field as the charge builds; no lightning is visible. In frame 2, a little flash, called a "leader," appears in the sky. Notice that this flash does

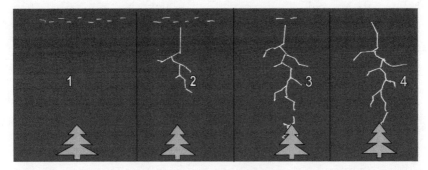

Figure 2.1. How an Electrical Field Produces Lightning. In frame #1, the field builds up. The sky has a negative charge, and the tree becomes positively charged. Then in frame #2, lightning begins, and so on.

not yet reach the ground. Perhaps you have seen such little flashes on a summer evening. The flashes occur, but lightning does not yet strike. In frame 3, a flash from the ground or a tree—called a "streamer"—makes a move, coming to meet the "leader." The leader and the streamer connect in square 4, and lightning occurs.

Likewise, the processmind is a field between the parts of ourselves, and between us human beings and everything else with which we connect. That space "between" seems empty until we are provoked to send verbal, auditory, or visual signals between parts, people, or the environment. Yet it may be connected to, and in fact may even provoke or "dream up," those communications.

Before going to bed at night, notice the atmosphere within and around yourself. Notice if little "leaders" and "streamers"—what I call "flirts"—catch your attention. They are expressions of the "emptiness" of the processmind and often turn up in dreams.

Likewise, be aware of the atmosphere of the relationship before you actually communicate with someone. In relationships, communication signals are like lightning. Just as lightning is preceded by "leaders" and "streamers," so our human signals are always preceded by "flirts"—subtle signals, tiny twitches, and impulses that don't quite make it to our everyday consciousness. Unless we train our awareness, we don't notice these communication "flirts"; that is, we ignore the "tension" in the field between us. Normally, we focus only on the "lightning" as it strikes. Then we say, "Ah-ha!" or "I dreamed this or that!" Or we characterize relationships as "You did this! What a statement!" or "You did this, and then I did that." Most of the time, we act as if we did not feel or sense what was coming next.

Without training your awareness, you may not notice the field situation that was present before the lightning came into being. That field is invisible; you can't see it with your physical eyes. In a way, it is "nothing." But this "nothing" can be *felt*. When two people are involved, I call this invisible field between them the relationship's processmind. Individuals, couples, groups, and, in principle, the whole world have processminds that characterize the spaces and atmospheres, the feeling and dreaming everyone shares. If we had more field awareness, we would not be so surprised by the big shocks in life, organizations would be better prepared for the future, and nations would not be so stunned by good luck or even bad luck, such as "sudden" attacks or natural catastrophies. If you are in touch with the processmind's field, you may be able to discern things before they occur.

EXERCISE 1: AWARENESS TRAINING

Give yourself a chance now to experiment with your processmind. To begin with, just feel whatever you imagine to be the power or field around yourself. Can you feel something trying to move you in one way or another? Trust you own experiences of that field. I recommend that you record your experiences with this exercise on the collage pages in appendix B, square #1.

Then, when you are ready, try following your body in the following manner: Half close your eyes and listen to your breathing. Wait until you have a sense of your body. Then, when you are ready, sense the direction in which your body tends to move or is trying to move. Follow this tendency. Move in the direction your body tends to move until you know why you are moving in that direction and what is trying to express itself. If you get a tip about why your body wants to move you in that direction, you know more about yourself; you are in touch with your momentary psychology or process.

In this exercise, how do you personally understand or describe the field that is moving or trying to move your body? Is that a power, or is it your "biology"? Is it some form of gravity; is it "God"? All those terms describe aspects of the processmind, the "mind" behind your "process," your spontaneous dreams and movements. Notice that when you are aware of that field and follow it, you may feel more "together." If you can sense the meaning of what the field is doing, your present life situation may take on more meaning.

Now let me pose another question, one that may not have one answer. "How does that field know where to move you at a given moment? Is it your psychology, your biology, physics, chance . . . or what?" My own answers to these possibilities are: yes, yes, and yes. I sum all these factors up by calling the thing moving you your processmind, the consciousness or field appearing as the dreams you have at night and as the body signals you notice during the day.

The processmind appears to you most frequently as a feeling or mood that precedes signals and events mirrored in your physiology. From the work of neurophysiologist Benjamin Libet we know that an electrical field precedes our voluntary or conscious control of anything we do, even when we say no to taking that action.[2] A field precedes our voluntarily taking any action. The processmind is the organizing field, a form of "power" that can in part be measured, the field in which you live with everything else.

WHY WE'RE NOT AWARE

If the processmind is so central—if knowing this field, this "dark sky," is essential to enlightenment, as Suzuki implies in the quotation at the beginning of this chapter—why are we not conscious of it all the time? One answer is that nature has given us the ability to marginalize our awareness of fields, to ignore or forget them. In quantum physics terms, the act of observing or measuring things collapses the wave function and creates reality. We can say, as it were, "I see and do this or that. I don't like fields, wave functions, or enlightenment! I don't want to know or believe in that stuff. I want to be my own boss!" As the expression goes: "Out of sight, out of mind."

Our ability to reject deep experience is in fact important to our overall nature as humans. This rejection separates us from our deepest nature, creating diversity, a world of many parts, and the possibility for reflection—that is, self-reflection! And saying "no" to the essence level of our experience allows us to focus more on visible signals and the tangible, consensual realities of the world. Thus, separation from the processmind gives us the ability both to create a consensus reality *and* to reflect upon what we experience—including the spaces between heaven and earth, between our own internal parts, and between people and things! Separation leads to the possibility of observation, including the possibility of noticing the processmind field between the observer and observed.

Because a processmind field precedes anything at which we look, our observation of something is actually entangled, or connected, with that thing, as well as with the field between observer and observed. I love the sketches of the universe by the great physicist John Wheeler. One of them, which I redraw here (see figure 2.2), shows the universe looking at itself through us. The universe, the U in the figure, is not just the sum of all things but also the space, the processmind, between us, looking at itself.

Figure 2.2. The Universe as a Processmind
Looking at Itself. Drawing inspired by a sketch by
physicist John Wheeler.

EXERCISE 2: PROCESSMIND AS BODY TENDENCIES

Let your own body explain more about the processmind as you do this second exercise, which involves shifting back and forth between everyday consensus reality and awareness of the processmind. Let's first start with your everyday reality. How do you normally identify yourself these days? With what type of "work" or job do you most identify? Think about that job for a moment. What feelings do you notice about that work?

Now once again, let's explore your experience of the processmind field in the form of movement tendencies. While standing or sitting, try to relax while retaining your body awareness. Relax so much that you feel as if you are almost sleeping, even though you may still be standing or sitting. Now when you are ready, while still in this "almost sleeping" state, with your lucid mind notice the movements your body tends to make. Notice its slightest tendencies to move. Follow them for a minute or two. Then, when you are ready, come back to your normal state of mind.

Repeat the entire experiment a second time, beginning with identification with your everyday reality. Continue "sleeping" and "waking" until you have the sense of how and why your body is moved about by the subtle tendencies of some field. Can you formulate in your own words what the nature of this field is? Can you sense the field's message? While still lucid, try to sense if this processmind has a purpose. Make a sketch and/or notes about your experiences in square #2 in the collage pages in appendix B.

One of my clients who had been severely depressed tried this exercise and found that his body movements and tendencies again and again made him experience that there was a wise hand moving him and that his life was not as hopeless as he had feared. The purpose of the depressing feelings was apparently to get him to drop out of everyday reality and sense this "hand," a new and deeper part of himself.

What I am calling the processmind is what you may be calling your mind, your unconscious, your deepest self, your biology, your dreambody, your wisdom, or even God.[3] When you are deeply in touch with it, you can sense it as something tending to move you. At any moment you can close your eyes, feel your body, and just notice where you tend to move. If you follow your body process, you can get to know your processmind as a field that is trying to "dream" you in some direction. That processmind precedes your dreams, just as an invisible field precedes lightning.

This reminds me again of what Suzuki Roshi says in the epigraph at this chapter's opening: "When you know everything, you are like a dark sky. Sometimes a flashing will come through the dark sky. After it passes, you forget all about it, and there is nothing left but the dark sky."

THINGS TO THINK ABOUT

1. The appearance of lightning strikes is preceded by an electromagnetic field. Notice tendencies and explore what is behind them.
2. Noticing your processmind as a field is a kind of enlightenment.

CHAPTER 3

ZEN METASKILLS

The processmind has been given many names through history, depending upon the culture and the times. The European alchemists, perhaps following the lead of the sixteenth-century alchemist Gerhard Dorn, spoke about the "Unus Mundus," the one world from which everything has come. C. G. Jung found this term during his studies of alchemy and used it in his own work to describe the hypothetical source behind all events in everyday reality. Jung called events that connected without an identifiable cause "meaningful coincidences" or "synchronicities."[1] I understand Jung to mean that the observer and observed emerge from the same source, the Unus Mundus.

As we have seen, the Zen Buddhist concept reflected in Suzuki's "dark sky" refers to the power and potential of the processmind. The earlier Zen Buddhists spoke of the essence level of our psychology in terms of the "Buddha mind." Most creation myths when speaking of the first moments of creation, before there were plants, rocks, fish, animals, and people, point to an inherently intelligent processmind field. For example, the Zulus of South Africa describe their mythic creator, Unkulunkulu, as a personification of the first "seed" from which the world was created. The early Chinese, when pondering the mysterious field out of which all change emerges, spoke of the "Tao that can't be said." This is the "Mother of heaven and earth." "Follow the Tao," they said.

I loved the idea of the Tao and wanted to learn how to follow it. However, it was so intuitive, I developed a kind of Tao-work, known today as process-oriented psychology. The processmind is a next step, adding a human element to quantum physics and its wave functions and an observer element to the Tao.

Even though the processmind is a general principle, each of us has our own processmind, as does every relationship, group, and organization. While an electric field can form and lightning appear anywhere on earth, the nature of the earth at a particular spot determines the way lightning appears there. So also, each processmind field has its own characteristics. You can sense the field around others. You can almost recognize a friend coming down the street on a dark evening because he or she has a certain "radiance" or "aura." Thus sensing the processmind is one of our deepest feeling skills. However, most of the time, we are unaware of this power, which is a power of the processmind to sense itself. My wife and partner, Amy, who wrote a book called *Metaskills: The Spiritual Art of Therapy*, might call this power a "metaskill."

In a way, metaskills are the heart of the processmind. A metaskill is the *way* you use your tools, the *way* you use concepts and skills.[2] For example, everyone uses a hammer at one time or another. The hammer represents a skill: pick it up, hit a nail on the head. But each person uses the hammer differently. When one person picks up a hammer, he or she looks like a carpenter. Another will look like a dancer, another like a boxer, and so on. The skill is the same, but each person does it in a characteristic manner, which is his or her own "metaskill."

Likewise, one Zen master who knows her own "dark sky" may be a stern master, the next may be a funny comedian, and so on. If you know your processmind, you also know your most powerful way of dealing with all kinds of situations. You need skills, but how you use them in life depends upon *metaskills*. The right skill with the wrong metaskill does not work as well as it could. The following exercise will give you a sense of your deepest self, that is, your processmind, and its particular metaskills.

EXERCISE 3: THE PROCESSMIND IN YOUR BODY

This exercise is best done standing, but any position will do. To begin, just scan your body, noticing and exploring any body sensations that come to your attention.

Take a moment to notice and follow your breathing. When you are perceiving how your breathing happens automatically, then find, feel, and imagine the deepest part of yourself in your body. Where might this self be in your body? You may feel it everywhere or in one spot or in several spots, or even around your body. Where does your experience tell you the deepest part of your self is? Now try to locate it in one area of your body. Perhaps it is in your head, your feet, your pelvis, your tummy, or your chest.

Wherever it is, feel the deepest part of you there. "Breathe into" that area and notice how your breathing brings out the nature of that spot more vividly. This is a very proprioceptive and intuitive experience.

As you breathe into the deepest part of yourself, let the experience that arises move your whole body a little bit. It may move you in subtle or more obvious ways. Some people need to give themselves permission to be moved by the experience arising from their deepest selves. Continue to breathe into that area of your body, and take time to experiment with "being moved."

When you have a clear sense of that movement, make a quick "energy sketch" of your movement experience in appendix B, on the collage pages under #3. Then look at that sketch. If a few words come to describe it, write them down. I call this experience and the sketch—this momentary appearance of the deepest part of you—the "processmind in your body."

How is your energy sketch typical of the energy or field that you radiate? Have others mentioned this about you? How is this energy typical of you? In other words, in what sense does your sketch represent one of your most basic feeling skills? Even if you do not consciously use this processmind metaskill much in the way you deal with life, you may still know it about yourself.

You may find yourself wishing you would use your process-mind metaskill in your life more often. It is likely one of your most powerful feeling metaskills—something in and around you that moves you and others.

For example, a typical metaskill of mine—one I have not always been conscious of or used congruently—is a gentle rising and falling motion, as if water were flowing around a rock. For me, this image represents stillness in the midst of motion (see figure 3.1).

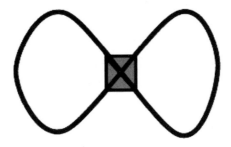

Figure 3.1. Rock with Flow Around It.
A processmind energy sketch.

PROCESSMIND BODY LOCATIONS

The processmind may not always be located in the same body spot. Some people locate their processmind spot in the head behind the eyes, some find it in the neck. Others find the processmind in the sternum, the heart, the solar plexus, at the base of the spine, or in their legs and feet. And some find it in the belly or lower abdomen. In Chinese and Japanese traditions, this region, known as the "hara," is often considered the seat of one's spiritual energy, or *qi*, and the goal of many spiritual teachings is to act from this center. Though the spot associated with processmind experiences may change over time, if you note the locations in the collage pages, you may eventually see similarities in your processmind experiences, similarities that have always been with you.

Frequently, people identify their processmind with a body area suffering from chronic symptoms. These symptoms may be "chronic" attempts by your processmind to manifest the experience of that body area. Do treat the symptom as a symptom, but you can also consider it a signal from your processmind, saying, in essence, "Don't forget me!"

THE PROCESSMIND'S METASKILL OF COMPASSION

The processmind is both a body experience of your deepest self and an energy or power that you radiate, perhaps unconsciously. As a field, this power precedes and organizes events, and its metaskill is the particular style or manner in which it does this. In my book *Earth-Based Psychology*, I discuss how Aboriginal people in various parts of the world ask the earth to show them in which direction to move. Not having maps and roads, our ancestors had to develop their relationship to the earth powers and let those powers show them "the way."

Those powers of the earth I am calling the processmind. As a field, it organizes the directions in which you should move at any given moment; it moves you this way and that way; it is always trying to "dance" you. You may have felt that a bit in exercise 3. The processmind moves you about just as the electromagnetic field between the earth and sky moves lightning flashes about and organizes them according to its "powers." Your insights, creative ideas, and spontaneity arise from that field.

At the very least, the processmind organizes your perception and awareness of events. At the most (as I show later), it organizes all the events of which you become aware. Get to know it. Use it so you can see for yourself if it is organizing or manifesting or making use of the events that take place. In many ways, the processmind's power and metaskill is probably the best way to deal with the events that are occurring in your life—and as I show in later chapters, the processmind of groups and organizations helps them best to deal with problems as well.

How does the processmind work as a metaskill? It organizes and "embraces" events in a compassionate or all-encompassing way. Compassion, as I suggested in *Earth-Based Psychology*, is the capacity to encompass all your signals, all your flashes, all your directions. In chapter 15 of that book, I discuss the relationship between compassion and the spontaneous directions you take in life. Applying this idea to the processmind, we can say that the processmind precedes, is the sum of, and has compassion for all your parts, phases, and directions in life. That is, the processmind is the "superposition" of all roles, phases, and periods of our lives.

SUPERPOSITION

Let me set aside the main topic of processmind for a moment to explain superposition, one of the processmind's characteristics. This mathematical term basically means adding one layer of something onto another layer. If there are several states in a quantum world, or you have several dreams during the night, the "superposition" of these states, or dreams, is their overall sum.

If each state or each dream part is represented by an arrow going in a particular direction, superposition means "adding" those arrows together. In more technical language, superposition "adds" vectors.[3] For example, in figure 3.2, if you superpose (or add) arrows 1, 2, and 3, you get the final arrow or vector U. U is the superposition of 1, 2, and 3. As I show in my book *Earth-Based Psychology*, 1, 2, and 3 could be individual dreams, directions, or feelings. U is simply the way a bird flies from the beginning point of 1 (marked by a plus sign) to the end of 3 (marked by an asterisk).

The processmind tends to pull you in a specific overall direction in life (the U), though at any given moment, it allows you to go in as many direc-

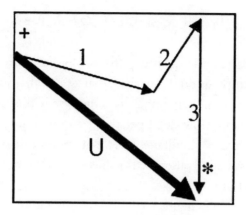

Figure 3.2. U as a Superposition of Arrows 1, 2, and 3.

tions as possible or as you would like (1, 2, and 3)—as long as they add up to your overall direction. Whereas 1, 2, and 3 are "free to be" and not predictable, the overall U course of your life is predictable. This direction corresponds to your deepest self, which in dreams may appear as your first memorable childhood memory, where it represents your personal myth.

That our childhood dreams tend to point out the overall direction of our lives is a remarkable fact and, I believe, also a mystery. Perhaps the processmind that organizes basic dream patterns and our overall direction is timeless. See chapter 5 of *Earth-Based Psychology* for more about U and compassion, that is, openness to all directions.

In any case, based on the math as a metaphor, we can say that the processmind's metaskill of compassion is able to appreciate each and every moment-to-moment zigzag in life. Just as the total sum of all your potential and possible directions is "open" to them all, regardless of which way they go, so too does your processmind embrace your diversity. It allows you to feel and appreciate two or more things at the same time, even if they are opposites. You can fight with and love someone at the same time. But to know this profound truth and live it in the best possible way, you need to be close to your processmind and not just your everyday self, which, as a part, is often in conflict with other parts.

IS THE CAT DEAD OR ALIVE?

One of the parents of quantum theory, Erwin Schrödinger, at first thought that since his quantum theory suggested that something could be in two states at the same time, as is the case with superposition, his theory was wrong. How can a person or a quantum system be in two very different states simultaneously? But indeed, quantum theory is right. The classic illustration of the dilemma is the paradox known as Schrödinger's Cat.

The illustration in figure 3.3 indicates the paradox. A cat is put inside a box, along with some poison that might accidentally spill and kill the cat, and the box is closed. According to quantum theory, until someone opens up the box to look, the cat is in a superposition of two states, both alive and dead. Once the cat is observed, the superposition of two states collapses into one state: either dead or alive.

Quantum physics is not really all that strange. In many ways it is like psychology, in that we can all be in two states of consciousness at the same time, though we usually favor one over the other. So also, you can be both alive (as a sleeping physical organism) and at the same time dreaming that you are dead, or even that you are standing at your own

Figure 3.3. Schrödinger's Cat. Before observation,
the cat can be both dead and alive at the same time.

gravesite looking at yourself in the grave! We know these paradoxical states of consciousness in day-to-day experience as well. We can behave in a "lively" manner even when we feel "dead" tired. Others may notice the secondary "dead" state in our double signals, for example, as signs of fatigue. Thus in a way, like Schrödinger's cat, we can be both dead and alive at the same time.

Perhaps all of nature has a processmind that allows everything to be in two or more states at the same time. Any shaman or child under the age of four will tell you that a tree is a tree and, at the same time, the tree is a talking spirit.

To explore superposition yourself, take a look at figure 3.4. At first you probably see either the white cup or the dark faces. However, if you relax your gaze long enough, you can probably see both kinds of shapes at the same time.

While our everyday mind focuses upon one state or another, our processminds are gazing and dreaming and, in a compassionate manner, are open to all states, paths, and directions. Your processmind is open not only to your everyday identity or "primary" process but also to your "secondary" or less conscious processes, with which you don't identify. Gestalt psychologists might refer to such processes as foreground and

Figure 3.4. Faces or Cup?

background. Although we normally split processes and focus only on one at a time, with a more sentient viewpoint it is possible to notice both states at the time and even the flow between them.

Using the Processmind as Metaskill

In terms of its metaskill, the processmind is not only a power or field behind a general life direction (U) but also the openness and compassion for all possibilities. Thus, the easiest way to deal with events is to experience them with the processmind, where yes, no, maybe, always, and never are all somehow present to greater or lesser degrees. From the perspective of the processmind, all events of which you are part are portions of a "whole" process or story.

For example, if two possibilities, A and B, arise, your everyday mind wonders which you should do. Your processmind would probably say, "Try all paths." In fact, even before you wonder which one, your processmind has already considered both paths (otherwise you could not have noticed them). It knows approximately where the stream called "you" is flowing—downward! Nevertheless, the specifics of how you go depend upon the stones and twigs, and the bugs and plants, in the path of the stream. The processmind's metaskill of compassion tries all the variations of the moment and embraces all directions, levels, and parts. You simply need to feel its gravity, remember the processmind, feel its pull, and let the moment direct you.

Soho's Sword

Takuan Soho (1573–1645), a legendary Japanese Zen master and major figure of the Rinzai Zen sect, said (in my words): Open up to your processmind. In his own words: "Not stopping the mind is object and essence. Put nowhere, it will be everywhere. Even in moving the mind outside the body, if it is sent in one direction, it will be lacking in nine others. If the mind is not restricted to just one direction, it will be in all ten."[4] If you are able to listen to processmind, you will not get stuck on any one event. For example, if you get caught in an argument, you will find yourself able to view the situation in a way that includes all sides.

According to Soho: "When the swordsman stands against his opponent, he is not to think of the opponent, or of himself, or of his enemy's sword movements. He just stands there with his sword which, forgetful of all technique, is ready only to follow the dictates of the subconscious. The man has effaced himself as the wielder of the sword. *When he strikes, it is not the man but the sword in the hand of the man's subconscious that strikes.*"[5]

I invite you to try Soho's suggestion. Let your processmind, your "subconscious," do things for you. Think of someone with whom you get into conflict. Express your own energy with one hand and the other person's energy with the other hand. Then relax for a moment and remember your processmind experience in exercise 3 in this chapter. Remember the feeling of the processmind in your body and the way it moved your body this way and that. Feel it moving your body now. Look at the sketch you made on the collage page in square #3.

Now imagine how your processmind state would deal with the energy of that someone (or something) with whom you are in conflict. To do this, stay close to your processmind experience; submit to it, so to speak, and notice how your processmind metaskill handles what you thought were opposing energies. Make a note in square #3.

If you use your processmind in disagreements, they become opportunities, and their courses may be very surprising! Nothing is a permanent problem, perhaps not even death. This reminds me of another story of Soho. In the last moment of his life, Soho painted the Chinese symbol for "dream," and then he lay down on the ground and died (see figure 3.5).

Perhaps he got close to his deepest dream, his processmind, and sensed its power—the "dark sky" Suzuki spoke of, the power that precedes all dreams and all events. By painting the symbol for "dream,"

Figure 3.5. Soho's Last Painting. The
Chinese pictograph for "dream."

perhaps Soho was telling us that beginnings and endings—even life and death—are only momentary situations from the perspective of our processmind. There is a larger direction that encompasses, but is more than, beginnings and endings.

Is it the timeless dreaming field that precedes both sleeping and awakening, a field that moves us in all situations, even death? Soho tells us that "it is not the man but the sword in the hand of the man's subconscious that strikes." Soho's metaskill was the power that moved his brush and painted "dream." The root of the Chinese and Japanese word for "dream," *mu* or *mushin*, has been translated as "the mind of no mind."[6]

THINGS TO THINK ABOUT

1. Your processmind is your sense of the deepest part of you in your body.
2. The processmind is your greatest metaskill, or way of dealing with many things, including fighting. This metaskill notices, embraces, and flows with all actions and events while remaining true to itself.

CHAPTER 4

THE POWER
OF YOUR PRESENCE

This chapter is an edited transcript of the author's class held at the Process Work Institute in Portland, Oregon, January 2009.

Today I want to speak with you about the field of the processmind in terms of your presence. But today I have a little cough. Perhaps I have the flu. Have you had the flu? (*Half the hands in the class go up.*) When I got up this morning, I thought, "I cannot do the class today. I have a little tickle in my throat and my mental state is altered from that flu." However, I then remembered dreaming in the night that this altered flu-like feeling was the *right* feeling; *it was the right way to go out in the world.*

I know what that means! My everyday mind can submit to the larger part of me, my processmind—that is, to the part of me that is speaking and healthy and at the same time coughing, fatigued, looking down, and moved by inner experience. I feel that my normal self can't do this class. It is up to my processmind. So my everyday mind may be a little less active than normal. If it is okay with you, every time I cough I will submit to the cough and also meditate and generally not put on too much of a public "appearance."

(*After pausing for a moment*) Today, my processmind feels and seems like a rock in the water. Mmmmm. (*Takes a minute or two and meditates on being a rock in water.*) Letting the water splash around me feels really good.

STUDENT:	We see that essence in you all the time anyway.
ARNY:	Yes, it is nothing new . . . is it?
STUDENT:	No.
ARNY:	It is a rock in the water. It was there before I got here. I sometimes deny it, but then I remember it. It's part of my presence. It's there even when I am sick, perhaps even when I am not even here.

PRESENCE

Your presence appears around you and also in the spaces and rooms you inhabit, as well as sometimes being associated with spots on earth. For example, my personal presence is—as I already said—like a rock in the water. This nature of your presence may be obvious to others, but it may well be distant from your consciousness.

Presence is a tertiary process. It is not primary—that is, it is not your identity process. It is not part of your secondary process—it is not part of the signals you emit but do not identify with. No, your process-mind and presence are at the third, more intuitive essence level. They are behind and, in a way, "prior" to all your signals. *Though everyone gets dressed up in consensus reality, your best presence—really, your most amazing self—is the processmind.* It is the subtlest and yet the most powerful force or energy that you possess.

If you don't know your presence, you may be confused about why people act toward you the way they do. Some will love you, and you may irritate others. The more you know about your own presence, the less confusing or irritating you will be. Why? Because the more you live your presence congruently, the less it has to "force" its way out. For example, if you have a shy presence and live it congruently, it becomes indisputable, like a beautiful forest flower. However, if you don't recognize your own shy nature, you look instead like a person who is acting related to others, while not really wanting to talk to anyone. Because other people perceive this disjuncture, they may be confused or criticize you for not really being with them.

Everyone should have their own definition of enlightenment. Some people call it connecting to love, others call it truth. Some say it is "empty mind." For me, enlightenment is knowing your processmind while being open to your everyday mind.

It's natural to lose touch with your deepest self as you enter and identify with everyday reality. Everyone has moments of detachment from ordinary reality and being in touch with processmind, then losing them, getting messed up, and then remembering the processmind again. Why all these variations and vacillations? My guess is that changing states of mind—being deeply in touch with our deepest self and then losing touch with that deepest self—is part of the diversity, part of the compassion or generosity, of the processmind. It obviously loves your everyday mind; that is why it's there so much! Few people are always detached from everyday reality—though I have met some people who have said they were!

What is presence exactly? What do we mean when we say "He blushed in her presence?" or "She sensed the presence of danger?" What does *presence* mean here? Why should I blush in somebody's presence? Everybody seems to know because a word for presence is found in every language I know of.

I suggest that presence is a *pre-sense*. *Pre* means "before," and *sense* means "feeling" or "perceiving" something. A *presence* is something you can almost feel before you can describe it as a feeling. Your processmind is a pre-sense. You need to know this pre-sense of who you are in order to be yourself, in order to facilitate your inner world and outer relationships, and even to improve world situations.

To be a good communicator of any sort, you must know your pre-sense. Otherwise it precedes you, and, as I indicated earlier, confuses communication. Your presence is like a kind of spirit that sends signals to others before you even know you've sent them! Think of teachers you loved. You may remember some of their words, but usually what moves us the most about such teachers is their presence.

If you know your own presence, you can even describe it to others. Knowing your own presence eases communication because it is there anyway, as an almost invisible signal behind all your other communications. If you identify only with what you do and say, you are likely to miscommunicate because that is not the whole of you.

For example, today one part of me is in a reduced state. In the moment, I am looking down at the floor and seeing nothing much down there, though looking down is familiar and soothing. My presence is connected with these "looking down" signals, with the earth at which I am looking. I am always a bit incongruent if I don't identify with that earth. Everything changes from day to day—our body pictures change, our intensity changes, we get older—but the processmind's presence may not change much over time. Presence is all around you.

SWIMMING IN THE SEA OF PRESENCE

One of my favorite stories about presence is called "The Little Fish." This is a Hindu story told by the Sufi master Inayat Khan.[1] Once there was a little fish. That fish goes to the Queen Fish and says, "I have heard about the sea, but what is the sea? Where is it?"

The Queen Fish explains to the little fish: "You live, move, and have your being in the sea. The sea is within and without, inside and outside, of you. You are made in the sea and you end in the sea. The sea surrounds you and is your own being."

The little fish says, "Huh?" (Actually, "huh" is not in Khan's story, I slipped it in!)

And the Queen says, "If you know the sea, you will never be thirsty."

We get thirsty, hungry, and needy if we don't know the sea, the field around us. Why don't we see it if it is all around us? Because it is a presense. It is the sea we swim in, the space we live in, the air we breathe. We are the sea, yet we identify with the fish and not the sea. The fish's presence is the power around it, as shown by the photograph in figure 4.1. The fish is wonderful, but the whole environment is as well.

For several hundred years, physicists have talked about the presence in which the parts of the universe "swim," so to speak, calling it *aether* or *ether*, the Greek word for "air" or "atmosphere." The aether was considered fieldlike. For some time, scientists thought aether was a medium that filled the entire cosmos and carried electromagnetic waves, a kind of presence in which all events were embedded.

Einstein at first disputed this notion, but later in his life he brought it back again, and today it is called the Einstein aether theory. Many physicists still propose that the universe is filled with a medium or field—some call it particle gravity, others refer to it as the "zero point" field, a kind of sea of virtual particles popping into and out of creation.

For Einstein, the aether was the essence of space time, a medium in which everything happened and which gave birth, as it were, to matter. In 1930 he said: "Now it appears that space will have to be regarded as a primary thing and that matter is derived from it, so to speak, as a

Figure 4.1. A Fish and Its Presence.

secondary result. Space is now having its revenge, so to speak, and is eating up matter."[2] Scientific theories still abound describing the space, the universe, in which we live as a medium or an energy that might give rise to everything else.

I call our experience of the physicist's aether a "presence," the mind of God, or our own processmind, which is both nonlocal, or universal, *and* has effects that can be localized in space and time. The processmind corresponds to something we all feel surrounding people and objects and that in some way gives birth to them.

We find similar ideas in Bohm's quantum potential theory, Jung's concept of the collective unconscious, Sheldrake's morphogenetic fields, Reich's orgone energy, yoga's prana, and Taoism's Tao and qi. An equivalent term can be found in most cultures on the planet. In earlier books, I speak about an "intentional field"—something that moves you with intent, which you can discover by meditating on your movements, as in the exercises in chapter 2.[3] The intentional field is a force field. In my *Quantum Mind and Healing*, I called the field around the processmind the force silence after *The Power of Silence*, a book title by Carlos Castaneda, the student of the shaman don Juan.

In all my previous books, I have been calling the world of space, time, and causality—the world we know in everyday life—consensus reality. The dreamworld, in contrast, is a timelike, spacelike world of subjective experiences, such as dreams, while the essence levels of awareness are nonduality-based experiences that seem to give rise to everything else.

ABORIGINAL AUSTRALIA'S DREAMING

The essence world is captured by Aboriginal people's feeling about the earth as a place of power or presence—not unlike Einstein's aether. For example, the Dreaming land of the Aboriginal Australian people is both the "real" land on which they walk with their feet and their subjective experiences of the "feelings" or "power" of the land—an essence quality.

The power of the earth is described often as a totem land spirit, which may be a real place, a field, or a power.

The oldest, longest-lasting spiritual and cultural history we know of belongs to the traditions of the Aboriginal Australian people. According to Professor W. H. Stanner, one of their proponents and researchers, these people believe in what he translates as "everyway."[4] For them, Dreaming is an objective reality that gives rise to objects and people all at once in physical reality. Objects such as kangaroos have a presence called "kangaroo Dreaming." They talk about Dreamtime as a presence and creative power.

According to Stanner, the Aboriginal Australians consider everyday time to be subjective. To follow a clock is *subjective*. Whereas Dreaming is closer to their objective consensus reality. Aboriginal people can feel presences; they know the Tao, the Dreaming, the processmind field of individuals and communities. They say that everybody can feel the presence of Dreaming. Space and time and today's consensus reality are also accepted by these people. Yet there is also a consensus about the reality of Dreamtime. They believe that there is a portion of every person that exists eternally, that was there before the person was born and continues after life ends. What I call presence, they would have referred to as the totem spirit.

YOUR EARTH SPOT AND ITS TOTEM SPIRIT

According to many Aboriginal mythologies, when your mother was pregnant, she may have walked by a tree or a cave or a little river in her fifth month of pregnancy. From that tree or cave or river, you—as a totem spirit—jumped out and into her womb. That is how you got here today. You are the totem spirit of a given place, its Dreaming or processmind. Imagine that! When your mother was in her fifth month, with her big tummy, the Dreamtime of that place emerged and became a person. Why the fifth month? That is the time when you started to wiggle in the womb.

According to Stanner, for thousands of years the Aboriginal Australian people have felt that the earth is sacred; it is a real being and, in our present terms, dreamlike, alive, spirited. Today also, many people feel inspired or somehow touched, affected, when they walk by a tree or along the seaside or out in the desert.

Imagine having no current-day knowledge of human reproduction, and then put together your awareness that fetuses begin to wiggle and kick during the fifth month of pregnancy with a vivid belief in the earth as a living, sustaining organism. Thinking in those terms, it is understandable how people might believe that a particular earth spot was incarnating at that moment. In any case, there was (and in a few areas still is) a widespread belief that people are the incarnated spirits of places on earth.

You are not just your human genetic inheritance. If your mother was in the forest, perhaps you are a totem spirit of the forest. That spirit is your presence, your aether, your processmind. You are the presence or aura of a given piece of land, of a river or the sea, a totem spirit, a spontaneous creation that popped out of a piece of earth when your mama was in her fifth month (see figure 4.2). I am indebted to these wonderful people for this imagination of totem spirit presence because it has helped me to understand who we are as part of our real and Dreaming universe.

Aboriginal people experience directions from the earth; I call these directions *vectors*. These people felt connected to the nature of a place and identify their roots with totem spirits of the land.

In the book *Lame Deer, Seeker of Visions* we find similar earth-based concepts. Speaking of the Great Spirit, the Native American Lakota holy

Figure 4.2. The Spirit of the Sea and the Spirit of the Forest.

man Lame Deer says, "He makes people feel drawn to certain favorite spots on this earth where they experience a special sense of well-being, saying to themselves, 'That's a spot which makes me happy, where I belong.'"[5]

Today many people, even those not identified with Aboriginal ancestry, still feel that the earth "speaks" to them. Many people have felt that it is their task in life to be a custodian, a caretaker, of a particular countryside—perhaps where their mothers were standing when a totem spirit jumped into their wombs. Caring for that area is our job. The power and presence of that area is our home base, the equilibrium position to which we always return.

This is the same as saying that your processmind presence is your most stable equilibrium position. Your normal self is like a pencil standing on its point, as illustrated in figure 4.3. Give it a little shove and it falls. Its equilibrium position is unstable. Now consider a heavy picture hanging from a nail on the wall. If you give it a shove, it will swing a little, but soon it will return to its equilibrium position, its starting point. It has a more stable equilibrium than the pencil.

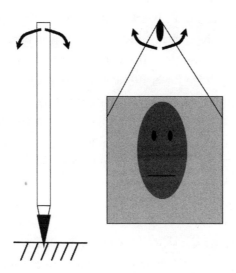

Figure 4.3. Unstable and Stable Equilibrium. The pencil is unstable and easily falls, but the picture swings and soon returns to its equilibrium position.

Your everyday mind is more like a pencil standing on its single itty-bitty point; it is less stable than your presence or processmind. Both of them vary, but the processmind swings about with fluidity, returning more predictably to its starting point.

In other words, centering yourself in your everyday mind is far more precarious than centering yourself in the processmind. Your everyday mind is easily destabilized by unpredictable events. In fact, even predictable events can send it toppling. The processmind, on the other hand, is focused on another center that allows it to "swing" with events, so to speak.

EXERCISE 4: PROCESSMIND AS STABLE PRESENCE

Let's explore your own sense of presence and its stabilizing effect. Sit or stand in a way that gives you access to movement, even micromovements, and ask yourself, as you did in the exercise in chapter 3, "Where in my body is the deepest part of myself?" Focus your breath on that area to amplify your sense of it.

Enjoy that sense for a moment, noticing the experience of your processmind in your body, amplified by your breathing. You might make sounds or motions that help you notice that feeling even more clearly. Observe the experiences, the sounds, and images that emerge. What kind of presence do they generate? What kind of presence is characteristic of this deepest part of you? Can you imagine it? Can you feel or hear it? Can you smell it?

When you have a sense of it, ask yourself, "With what kind of spot on earth, with what sort of place, might this presence be associated?" Feel the presence, let it move you, and associate the resulting experience with a spot on earth. There may be many several such places, but choose one for the moment. Now go to that spot in your imagination and look at it. Become that area. What is it like to be that earth spot? What power or presence does it have? Is it quiet or loud, dark or light? Is it vast or enclosed, high or deep? And so on. Make a note about the presence of that spot.

We can call that presence, which is the presence of your processmind, an experience of the totem spirit associated with that earth spot. Just enjoy that place. Let it move you, inspire you. What is the difference between the feeling you get from this spot and the feeling you have during your ordinary day being your normal self?

Your processmind, or the totem spirit of that earth spot, is probably something that is most typical of you over long periods of time, the place that feels best or feels like "home." You may return there often. It may be your most stable spot, perhaps one you have always been seeking. Make a note about this presence in appendix B, on #4 of the collage pages at the end of this book.

Now, consider how you normally identify your ordinary self. Then look around your processmind earth spot. Where would your normal identity fit into what you experience there? For example, if you feel that your everyday mind self is rigid, perhaps you find it in rocks near that earth spot. Or if your everyday self is sweet, perhaps you find a flower in that spot. Look around that processmind area and appreciate its diversity, even if it is in the desert. That area is your presence.

KNOWING YOUR PRESENCE

People who love you probably love your presence. But think of your ex-friends. Perhaps they liked your everyday self but then were upset by your processmind, which they did not quite see. Think of somebody who did not like you very much. If you had known your presence at the time and stated it clearly, would that have helped avoid difficulties? You probably related to this person with your everyday self and then surprised him or her with your true presence. Usually we relate with only one part of ourselves, and our presence is not brought into the relationship clearly enough. If you bring your presence in more clearly, it might make things easier.

For example, many years ago, I fooled myself and a couple of friends by acting only like my normal parental self. That is a big part of me, but it is not me entirely. There is something else larger, something like a bear. *Grrr*! It is more like waves crashing on the rocks at the seashore. *Woof*! Those friends, who did not know me very well, were also surprised to find that *woof*!

STUDENT: My processmind is a void, the empty space between my chest and my gut—the deepest, most unknown part of me. When I am in relationship, that emptiness sometimes pops out spontaneously, like from a cave in the ground. Something comes out that I don't identify with and gets me into trouble. I feel okay, but others are shocked.

ARNY: You had better say to others, "My presence is a vast, unpredictable emptiness out of which anything can emerge." Tell them, "I am a process, a void out of which stuff pops. I'm not just the stuff itself."

STUDENT: Yeah, I see, and if somebody loves the void, they will love me. They will love the unpredictable cave.

YOUR PRESENCE IN THE SPACES YOU INHABIT

Remember your processmind. Imagine it. When I imagine the processmind's field and presence, I sometimes think of an amazing picture from the Bread and Puppet Theater. It features a larger-than life puppet with an enormous face against a background of trees with an ordinary person playing a bass violin at the bottom of the frame. Whereas in everyday life we focus on the person playing the bass violin, the dreamer and artist in us knows that the processmind is in the dreaming sense we get from the entire forest background, possibly symbolized by the looming figure behind the musician.

The power of the particular earth spot that is associated with your processmind emerges from that earth area, organizing aspects of your nature, including your behavior in relationships. Indeed, it organizes your whole life—even the spaces and the atmosphere of your favorite personal room.

Just look around your own room at home—your favorite room or corner of a room. Can you see that room in your mind's eye? What is it like? What is the color of the room, and what materials are in it? What is in front of you, to the side, and in back of you? What do you see through the window? What is most characteristic about this room that you love the most? What is its atmosphere like? And how does that connect to your totem spirit and earth spot?

Figure 4.4 is a representation of what might be a college student's room, with a coffeepot, a bulletin board, a bookcase, a poster on the wall, and lamps and chairs and books and papers all around. Think about how you have organized the rooms in which you have lived. You have probably tended to organize them more or less the same way again and again as you moved from house to house, apartment to apartment, city to city. Your processmind or earth presence serves as the architect of your physical space.

When you go to a park, a theater, or somebody's house, you are in the presence of that place. When you walk into someone's room, you are walking into someone's mind, their processmind, their power spot. I have talked about the processmind as a field that moves you, as a force behind your metaskills. Now I hope you sense it in your presence as a totem spirit, as a piece of the earth that also organizes the world in which you live.

Figure 4.4. College Student's Room. What power organized it?

THINGS TO THINK ABOUT

1. Everything changes, but your presence is the most stable aspect of you. This processmind, this essence, is the "sea" in which you live.
2. Native peoples associate the processmind with a particular earth spot and the invisible power that emanates from that spot. This power organizes all of your living spaces.

CHAPTER 5

YOUR PROCESSMIND, THE TAO, AND BABY TALK

In preceding chapters I have indicated that the processmind organizes our overall direction yet also allows us to zigzag in life according to the needs and choices of our everyday mind. Thus life is "self-organized" and predictable at the largest scale but free and indeterminate in moment-to-moment events—up to a point, since these moment-to-moment events seem to be constrained by the invariant overall U direction. If you can sense the overall direction of the processmind, then a momentary movement in another direction—even the opposite of your overall direction—is acceptable or even fine. However, if you don't sense the processmind and are identified only with your everyday self, you are far more likely to feel conflicted about the momentary direction to move, whether large scale or small scale. In this chapter I will talk about the processmind in terms of directions, but first I must discuss its wave and particle nature. Then we shall see how processmind appears in the I Ching and in the language of babies.

The processmind has at least two characteristics. First, it is field-like; it can be felt but not easily verbalized. Second, it is particle-like. You can see, hear, feel, smell, and sense a specific something like a body tendency, a dream image, a "flirt," or a directional movement.

The Tao is similarly described as having two natures. The first line of a most ancient and basic Taoist text, the Tao Te Ching, says "The Tao that can be said is not the real Tao." But then the text goes on to describe the

Tao in many ways. For the Taoists, the Tao is "the mother of heaven and earth," the source of all creation.

This dual nature, both field and particle, of both the Tao and the processmind again reminds me of the quantum wave function, a pattern that cannot be seen or "said" (because it is a complex number, that is, a number that is both real and imaginary) but constrains and gives rise to an infinite number of possible paths.[1] The sum total of all these paths is the one we are most likely to see in the reality of space and time.

What you see depends upon the nature of yourself as the observer. The perception of a particle in quantum physics depends upon the way the physicist looks at it. If you are a physicist, and you shoot a particle through one slit, it behaves as if it were a particle of sand. As more and more particles are shot through the slit, a cluster of particles, looking a bit like a little pile of sand, builds up beneath the slit at the bottom of the box (see the left-hand side of figure 5.1). If there are two slits in the screen, such that a particle could travel through either one (see the right-hand

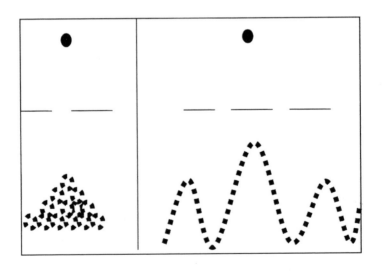

Single Slit Pile Up   Double Slit for Quantum Particles

Figure 5.1. Double Slit Experiment.

side of the figure), you might expect particles to pile up and to see two piles of "sand" at the bottom of the box. But no! Instead you get a wavy pattern. If the particles are shot through one opening, they behave as particles and pile up like sand. But if they are shot through two openings, they pile up more or less as if they were waves. Quantum stuff appears as both particles and waves depending upon how they are observed.

Psychology agrees that what you see depends upon the nature of the observer, that is, on how you look at it. For example, if you focus on the sense of God as something moving you, you might experience that God as a field, such as gravity. If you wait for an image, you may experience God as a humanlike figure or part of the human world. If you look at what Jung called the "unconscious" (and I call the "processmind") as it appears in dreams when you are asleep, it may seem to be a powerful field or particular image. However, if you look at it in the body, it appears as body tendencies, directions, or even body symptoms—that is, in far more "down-to-earth" guises. In religion the unconscious or processmind might be portrayed as a mythic figure in the sky. In science it seems like the mystery behind waves and particles.

The processmind is similar. What it looks like depends upon your state of mind when you look at it. There is the processmind of which we can speak—that is, that appears as dreams, body experiences, or earth spots—but it is not the total picture of the processmind. And there is the field-like aura from which all these things that can be spoken of emerge. In a way, the processmind's field-like aura is like the Tao that cannot be said.

THE TAO

For the ancient Chinese, the Tao was a kind of "unified field theory" spanning heaven and earth. Early Taoists understood that the Tao manifested spontaneously in events or directions. To know what to do next, their guideline was, "Follow the Tao." And they developed specific techniques for determining the Tao.

Using one of the world's most ancient divination procedures, recorded in the I Ching or "Book of Changes," the early Taoists tossed sticks or flipped coins to identify what they called *yang* and *yin* energies, depending upon which side of the coin turned up.[2] The Tao that "can't be said" was understood to express itself in the way the coins fell; the Tao could be understood as a kind of field behind these spontaneous events, much like the dark sky is a field preceding the lightning. (See my *Earth-Based Psychology*, appendices 9, 10, and 11, for details about the I Ching, the big U, and vector thinking.)

According to how the coins flipped, they created "trigrams," composed of different trios of solid (—) and broken (– –) lines, representing yang and yin energies respectively. With these they derived hexagrams, composed of two trigrams, one superposed upon the other. For example, the left-hand image in figure 5.2 shows hexagram number 27 in the I Ching, called "The Corners of the Mouth," or "providing nourishment."

In chapter 42 of the Tao Te Ching, the Tao is summed up as the "Taiji" or universal field: "Tao manifested as *One*, which is Taiji." The Taiji sym-

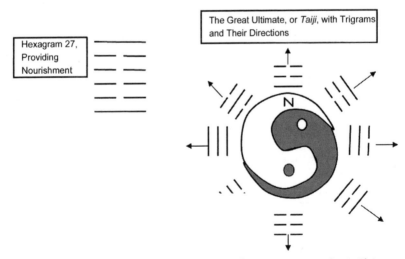

Figure 5.2. Trigrams, Hexagrams, and Directions in the I Ching.

bolizes the source from which all things flow, a grand unifying field that was present in the beginning of the universe. On the right side of figure 5.2 you see the circular form representing the Taiji, or Tai Chi, the Great Ultimate, the potential source out of which all things emerge. The eight possible forms of the trigram placed around the Taiji correspond to the eight directions: north, northeast, east, southeast, south, and so on.

Since a given "Tao," or hexagram, is the sum of two trigrams, the Tao, or "Way," is, in principle, the sum (or superposition) of two directions. (I speak about this in detail in appendix 8 of *Earth-Based Psychology*.) In figure 5.3, I have added together the two direction vectors (north and northeast) associated with the trigrams that make up hexagram 27 to show the hexagram's overall vector direction—the Tao's direction, represented by the bold line— which you can read about in the I Ching under that hexagram.

Why am I showing all this vector stuff to you, dear reader? The same idea of vector sums implied in the Taoist thinking of thousands of years ago is found in the math of quantum theory today. Just as the overall pattern (or quantum wave function) is the sum of separate states, so is the Tao is the sum of two or more states. I would also suggest that quantum physics and Taoism are both indications of a more general processmind pattern, a field-like power moving us moment to moment through what otherwise seems like accidental events and random directions.

Like the Tao, the processmind is an invisible field behind the directions. The concept of the processmind is an update of the concepts of the quantum mind and the Taoist mind—the "Taoist mind" being the

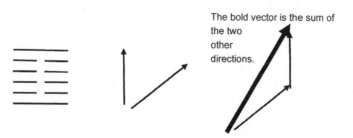

The bold vector is the sum of the two other directions.

Figure 5.3. Hexagram: The Vector Sum of Trigram Directions.

mind of the Taoist sage, which is connected to and can follow both the moment and the universe.

Physics describes fields partly in terms of lines of force, referring to the potential force that a field exerts upon an object in its neighborhood. The ancient Taoists described the Tao in terms of wavy field lines called "dragon lines." They developed an Chinese earth-based method, Feng Shui, to find land areas, burial sites, or places to live using the Tao's dragon lines. Feng Shui is the art of knowing how to align oneself or create harmony with the environment. A shaman might call Feng Shui the art of knowing where, when, and how to be in the best possible spot.

The Feng Shui method points to our human ability to know and be in touch with the Tao as an earth-based field, and to recognize the importance of adjusting ourselves and our spaces accordingly. The message is simple: Follow the Tao, the sense of the force field, to be at one with nature and with processes. Follow the processmind to be at one with what is happening.

THE EARTH'S MAGNETIC FIELDS

An object such as an electric charge or a magnet has lines of force around it to indicate its influence on other objects. The earth itself is such a magnet with a field around it. The left-hand image in figure 5.4 shows an electromagnetic field sketched around the earth showing the field's lines of force. Where the lines are drawn close together, the force they exert on objects is stronger. Where the lines are farther apart, there is less force exerted on objects in the earth's field. Such field lines can be imagined as coming from the north and south poles of a magnet (see the right-hand image in the figure). In other words, our planet is, in some ways, a bar magnet. Flowing red hot metals in its core create its magnetic field. The earth's field is always in process, always shifting, and one day may even reverse itself. Magnetic north may become magnetic south in the future. Then you will have to think differently about your compass.

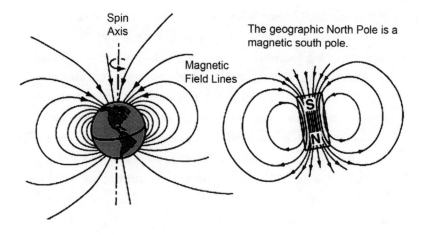

Figure 5.4. Earth's Electromagnetic Field. The earth's electromagnetic field is like the field of a dipolar bar magnet.

Force fields are concepts, mathematical ideas that allow scientists to visualize the effects of objects upon one another and give form to the essence-like fields. Long before we knew about the theory of magnetism, our ancestors understood that fields—the Tao, Taiji, gravity, and electromagnetism—move us. When we consider the earth's field, our imaginations help us understand its ineffable quality. We see lines of force, dragon lines, infinity, symmetry, emptiness, and so on. We sense fields objectively and/or subjectively.

EXERCISE 5: THE PROCESSMIND FIELD AROUND YOU

We have been discussing fields. Now let's explore your processmind field. What does the field around you look like? If you have a sense of your processmind field, you have a more complete picture of yourself than any photograph could show.

Get a piece of paper and a pencil and draw yourself as a stick figure. (Don't forget to sketch this figure into square #5 in appendix B at the end of this book.) Follow your breathing for a minute or two. Then, as you did in exercise 3, scan your body to find the deepest part of yourself, and when you have found it, breathe into that area.

When you are ready, sense the area around your body, whatever that may mean to you. While you are doing that, simultaneously look at your stick figure and let your hand quickly sketch the "field" of your deepest self as some sort of area or lines around your stick figure. Let your playful mind just sketch what you feel around your body. Your sketch might even surprise you.

When you have finished, explore that field. Look at it. Play with the idea that you are not only a body but *that field*. Then pretend you are that field and make little motions showing the field's motions. Notice the difference between being the field and being your normal self. Let your field move you a little bit; let it buzz or move in whatever way it wants. What is the nature of your field? Meditate on that. What does it teach your everyday self about your larger self?

For example, the stick figure with the field around it in figure 5.5 told the woman who drew it that she should spin

Figure 5.5. Processmind Energy Sketch:
Stick Figure with Field around It.

more in her life. She should not be linear like her stick figure but should swing and sway, be a little dizzy, and follow what she called the "heavens."

To know yourself as including your processmind field is to know what you truly look like. Your sketch is one of your "real" pictures.

SYNAESTHESIA AND BABY TALK

Now put that sketch aside, because I want to encourage you further to explore and describe your field using another method, synaesthesia. Let me first describe synaesthesia. When you awaken in the morning, you may have noticed that sometimes you feel that you are neither awake nor asleep. You are "half here and half there," in a synaesthesia mode of being in which thinking, speaking, feeling, moving, seeing, hearing, tasting, dreaming, and the rest of your senses overlap. Direct experience of the processmind is a "half here, half there" altered state as well.

Syn comes from the Greek term for "sum," and *aesthesia* is Greek for "sensation." *Synaesthesia* means, literally, "sum of the senses." Synaesthesia is a superposition of senses. Feeling and seeing can usually be separated, but in synaesthesia they overlap. Actually, most body symptoms are probably best expressed as a combination or overlapping of several senses. Think of a migraine headache, for example. Many people when they experience a migraine feel the pounding as if of a hammer and at the same time see and almost hear the migraine headache's "aura," or field, and its pain and buzz.

Some people see colors associated with certain forms, letters, and numbers. For example, synaesthetes may see the letter *S* as pink. When these gifted people read, they see colors or hear sounds as well. Some words are also associated with tastes. One of my clients used to forbid me from saying the word *inspiration* because it was too salty!

Everyone has access to this overlapping of senses. Take a look at figure 5.6. These two images were used by Gestalt psychologist Wolfgang Koehler to explain synaesthesia. He would ask: Which of these two shapes would you call "kiki" and which one "bouba"? "Kiki" is most often associated with the sharp image to the left and "bouba" with the soft one to the right.

We are all synaesthetes in the sense of associating shapes with sounds or body feelings with visualizations. Think, for example, of the English expression "Your shirt is loud" or "That situation just does not smell right." Synaesthesia is an essence aspect of how we communicate with one another. Babies partly communicate this way, which is probably why adults tend to make preverbal sounds, motions, and facial expressions when speaking to little kids. For example, some babies appear to associate certain kinds of sounds with the sensation of being embraced.

Now let's return to exercise 5. Take a look at your sketch of the field around the stick figure representing your body. Now allow yourself for a moment to be a baby. Go back to the time before you had words and experiment with feeling a bit like a baby. Use baby talk: "guu, guu, kiti," and so on. Remember that "guu, guu" period of life.

Now look at your picture and try to describe it in baby sounds and baby motions. Express your field as a baby might. Then, when you are ready, dance and sing your field—whatever that means to you. Finally, name that field and express your experience in words. Have courage— just make baby sounds and motions, dance movements, and finally express all this in words.

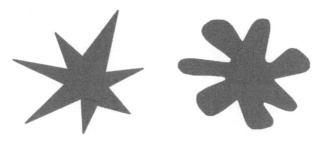

Figure 5.6. Two Drawings Demonstrating Synaesthesia.
Which is "kiki" and which is "bouba"?

Your sketch and the sounds and movements you make might remind you of childhood experiences or allow you to understand some of your behavior as a child. Did this processmind field experience appear somewhere in your childhood? How has this field been trying to appear in your dreams, in your body, in your relationships, and in your life context? Be this processmind field experience and give yourself some advice, especially about things on your mind. Finally, don't forget to record your sketch and notes in appendix B, square #5.

When my wife, Amy, did her processmind field sketch (see figure 5.7), she quickly drew a bundle of wavy lines around herself and said her aura was "fuzzy, warm, and magical." She said, "I am the processmind, a sweet little magician with *ooogooshu* sounds. Loving magic is my way." Amy acted and spoke at the same time, talking to herself, "You sweet little thing, you can fly! If you love yourself and go inside, you can do anything." Amy then commented, "Wow, that sounds like my 'way.' When my inner critic shows up, I don't need to deal with him in an ordinary manner. I should just do magic on him!"

Your processmind has specific powers and metaskills. It has presence and direction. It seeks to know itself in terms of your dreams and

Figure 5.7. Amy's Processmind.

the spots on the earth that you seek, in terms of your room, your Tao, your field, and even in baby talk! Wherever you go, remember your processmind. It is the big picture appearing as a field, as a direction, as the overall power; it is the "map" that shows the way.

THINGS TO THINK ABOUT

1. Quantum wave functions, magnetic fields, the Tao, the Taiji, and the earth's Feng Shui power are all aspects and metaphors of the processmind's lines of force.
2. Your processmind may be best expressed in baby talk.

PART TWO

THE PROCESSMIND IN SYMPTOMS, RELATIONSHIPS, AND THE WORLD

All of you are perfect just as you are,
and you could use a little improvement.

— Shunryu Suzuki Roshi

HOW YOUR SIGNATURE FIELD MASTERS PROBLEMS

In the first part of this book, I discussed specific qualities of your processmind and presented various inner-work exercises that help to reveal these qualities. In part two, I want to show you how to use your processmind field experiences to deal with relationship issues and personal, body, and world problems. This chapter, in particular, shows you that the "signature field" of your processmind is not just the lines of force around you (as we saw in the previous chapter) but the feeling you associate with certain places on earth. The chapter also describes how you can use this association to deal with your own moods.

MARGINALIZATION

If the processmind is the guiding intelligence behind life, why do we need to do anything to apply it to our lives? Is it not already operating on everything? Yes, the processmind seems to be the intelligence organizing the processes and events we meet during our day and nighttime lives. But in everyday life the processmind also marginalizes the mystical or imaginary parts of itself. Why? A quantum physicist would say the reason is visible in the math. Observation "collapses" the superposition of several possible states into one, and only one, state. This is just the way our nature, indeed all of nature, operates. When we observe ourselves, most often we identify with our body, our problems today, and what might happen tomorrow. Our deepest self and its various states seem to collapse as if they were "just a dream."

Is there a purpose behind this marginalization? I don't know the answer for certain, but I can point out that when the superposition collapses, we identify with the observer and not with the observed, which seems to be "outside" of us. This reminds me of the physicist John Wheeler's image of the universe as a huge whale that bends and looks at its own tail (see figure 6.1). We human observers, standing in the present moment on the earth, feel that the universe is *way out there*, its farthest edge 13.7 billion light-years away, and is not us! However, with a deeper processmind perspective we realize that we are one part of the whale (the universe) observing our other parts. We are our families, friends, communities, nations, the planets, and the universe that is constantly discovering itself. As we move along in this book, I will show how this perspective can help us to resolve problems on many different levels.

In a way, the processmind needs our everyday mind, our infamous "ego" or primary process in order to objectify itself. Marginalization of our dreamlike and quantum nature allows us to observe, measure, and create reality as if it were not us. However, the ongoing feeling that the other is

Figure 6.1 The Universe Looking at Itself.
Inspired by a sketch by physicist John Wheeler.

"not me" and in conflict with "me" eventually becomes uncomfortable. Even worse, this consensus reality viewpoint is self-depressing. Depression implies that something is pressing on the everyday mind. Often, relief lies in getting to know or integrating what is doing the depressing. Sometimes relaxing, letting go, giving in, or going "down under," in the sense of feeling the earth, can be very helpful for a depressed mood.

How the Earth "Under-Stands"

Understanding means literally "standing under." In a very concrete way, the earth is the common "under-standing" of everything occurring on its surface. Thus earth experience becomes essential for both our inner and outer processes. From my work with individual, interpersonal, organizational, and world conflicts, I have come to realize how important this sense of the earth's "under-standing" can be. In fact, I am amazed that it took me so many years to realize the crucial role of the earth's field in our psychology. This processmind experience of "under-standing" is what we need to address the problems facing the planet today. What a paradox! The earth can help itself.

Think about it. The earth was created about 4.5 billion years ago. The human race, according to a 1997 estimate, is roughly 1,000 to 10,000 generations old.[1] This means that the human race is about 200,000 years old. Human beings are newcomers to the planet. We are babies! Our earth, revered by the indigenous people of the Andes as the goddess Pachamama, often translated as "Mother Earth" or "Mother Universe," is our link to the universe. It is literally our common ground. We often fight over the borderline between "my" land and the land of the other person, forgetting our common connection to Pachamama. When I speak of our planet, I think of its interior, its crust, its valleys, forests, deserts, glaciers, waters, skies, cities, street corners, cafés—all as being both real and dreamlike. The earth's parts are simultaneously measurable places and fields that can be imagined as totem spirit figures and presences.

Signature Fields and Totem Spirits

In chapter 5, we saw that each of us has a particular presence or field. Associating this presence with a certain earth-based field creates what I call your "signature field," a consistent power that is a special characteristic of your nature. As humans, we all share the same "mother earth," yet each of us represents a particular part of her. The way you do anything is an expression of your signature field, the power moving you, the earth spot you "come from."

Figure 6.2 represents a visual sense of Einstein's possible signature field. I did not know Einstein personally, but I know he loved sailing. That is why I chose this picture of him sailing on Saranac Lake in the Adirondack Mountains in northern New York, a place he often went for rest and renewal. That lake area would reflect his interest in the earth and heavens, and sailing would express his sense of the relativity of motion (among the sailboat, wind, water, and earth). Perhaps such a place helped to enlighten Einstein about his own nature and the nature of the universe.

Figure 6.2. Einstein's Signature Field.
Einstein sailing on Saranac Lake.

We know from the story and representations of the Buddha's enlightenment under the Bodhi Tree just how important the earth underneath that sacred fig tree was. Judging by the frequent association of his enlightenment with this tree (as seen on the Internet alone!), we can say that this tree area was the earth-based signature field of his "Buddha nature" or "Buddha principle" (*Buddha-dhatu*). This nature and principle are "taught to be a truly real, but internally hidden potency or element within the purest depths of the mind, present in all sentient beings, for awakening and becoming a Buddha."[2]

Near the end of his enlightenment story, the Buddha was challenged by the great tempter Mara, the personification of all earthly passions, who was trying to claim the earth for himself. The Buddha, however, touched the earth, indicating that enlightenment could and would happen on the earthly plane, free of Mara.[3] In figure 6.3, you see the seated figure of the Buddha touching the ground with the fingers of his right hand. According to some stories, when the Buddha touched the ground, the earth responded with an earthquake, implying that yes, the earth belonged to the Buddha, not Mara.

It also seems possible that by touching the earth, the Buddha was saying that the earth was the point. The Buddha's true nature, his Buddha nature, is the signature field, the power emanating from the earth beneath himself and the Bodhi Tree.

Buddhists speak of enlightenment in terms of *nirvana*, a permanent consciousness of this Buddha nature. In the state of nirvana there is no ailing. Rather, there is equanimity and an end of cycling between life and death. In Japanese Zen Buddhism, this glimpse of one's true nature, of nature as it is, is called *kensho*. *Satori* is a more permanent form of enlightenment.

For me, knowing and identifying with the processmind is a form of kensho, nirvana, or satori. Everyone has moments of finding the processmind, or Buddha mind, and then losing it. Most people feel so good when they find their Buddha mind that when they lose it, their ordinary, Mara-like mind tells them they have failed in some way. But Mara is just

Figure 6.3. The Buddha Touching the Earth.

a part of the enlightenment process. Mara forces us to go "down," to get closer to the earth, and, from a process-work perspective, the Buddha is the one who realizes and is enlightened by that "downness."

The ways of achieving awareness of your true nature, that field of the "dark sky," vary depending upon the culture. Some cultures emphasize dreamwork, others follow their breath and meditate on something sacred or pray, and so on. For earth-based peoples, the Buddha mind is roughly analogous to the location on earth where they feel best or most at home. Knowing your processmind or earth-based "totem spirit" is a new experience for some, but it is also an ancient form of consciousness linked to the space surrounding and between things.

In chapter 4, I spoke of the Aboriginal Australian belief that when your mama was in her fifth month of pregnancy, a totem spirit jumped out of some part of the earth and into her body. This Aboriginal idea is one of the oldest mythological understandings of human beings and is one explanation for how you got here and who you are. It implies that every time you remember the land you love the most, you are "home." We are custodians and devotees of places on this earth. We find this identification with the land in native traditions everywhere. Native Americans and native Europeans alike named their children after places on earth. One Feather, Black Elk, Sun Bear, Woodland, Forrest, Berg, Stein, and so on are all names connected to the earth's objects or materials.

Exercise 6a: Your Signature Field

The goal of this exercise is to develop a meditative mindfulness practice focused upon your signature field, your earth spot. In the second exercise in this chapter, we will use your signature field to help you deal with bad moods. For this exercise, you will need some paper and a pen or pencil for making notes and sketching. Please don't forget to record both exercises in #6a and #6b on the processmind collage pages in appendix B.

As preparation, take a moment to sense the earth beneath you, the earth around you, whatever the earth means to you in the moment. Relate to it in any way that feels natural in the moment. Now note down on the paper the earliest memory or dream you can recall in life. Choose just one. Then put that note to the side. Stand up and move in place a little and feel the deepest part of yourself, whatever that means to you in the moment. Even if you did this in earlier exercises, approach this part of the exercise with a "beginner's mind," as if you have never done it before. The repetition may make your connection to your deepest part a more automatic and thus accessible process.

Where in your body is that deepest part of you just now? This is intuitive; trust your body to tell you where it is. Breathe into that spot and feel its quality and energy. Notice sounds that come from that spot. Perhaps a melody or even a song comes up now. Use all your senses and synaesthesia—that is, your overlapping senses—as you feel, move, and make sounds. For example, you may feel yourself breathing and making sounds like the sea, the wind, and so on. Sing and hum, feel and visualize your experiences.

When you are ready, ask yourself what spot on the earth, real or imaginary, you associate with this experience, sound, or vision. If many spots come to mind, pick one. When you are ready, go there in your imagination. Feel yourself being there, sense the presence or power of the earth connected to this place. Sense the field of this place, its presence and power. How would you describe it? Now, let this earth-based field and power move or "dance" you.

While moving or dancing, ask yourself if this field reminds you of anything in your earliest memory or dream. When you are ready, let a quick sketch of this field experience emerge in square #6a in the collage pages. Name it. This piece of land and its power are central aspects of your processmind's energy, your signature field.

Now be the field of that earth spot: feel its presence and power and then, with relaxed, open awareness, shape-shift—leave your human form for a moment—and allow yourself to imagine *being* the field. Take your time as you let the field move you. Notice your visions, feelings, sensations, impulses, and thoughts.

If at some point you get distracted, simply go back to your signature field energy and your sketch, and let that processmind field continue meditating while another part of you follows those distractions. Makes notes in square #6a about what you have learned about your signature field.

BAD MOODS

With your processmind in your consciousness, you probably feel more detached from everyday events and possibly more "in your body." Now let's use that processmind signature field to go further, to work with bad moods, by associating your worst mood with a direction on the earth. But first let me explain vectors.

When I showed vector work to an Aboriginal Australian elder, she said, "'Oh, very good, we have been doing this for years." The practice of following earth-based directions is ancient. Your body naturally knows about signature fields and vectors, even if the concepts are new to you. Trust your body to show you in which direction to go. Your own intuition, or dreaming body, will explain why you are going in that direction.

Some people move toward the actual north, south, east, or west and associate particular experiences with certain places in those directions. Others feel the direction in which they are moving is west, north, and so on, though according to the compass it is not. That is just fine. Your subjective experience of where you are going is the point. You may also find yourself simply going somewhere in a room, or toward a tree or picture—some place that just feels right. Whether it leads you to a tiny room or a place with a sweeping vista, trust the deepest part of you in your body to guide you in the direction that best serves you.

EXERCISE 6B: MOODS AND VECTOR WALKING

For this second exercise you will need two small pieces of paper. Mark one with a plus sign (+) and the other with a star or an asterisk (*).

We can use this exercise I call "vector walking" for just about any experience. But I want to focus here upon bad moods, because they are difficult experiences to deal with. Think of your worst mood or one that's been bothering you recently. Choose just one, the one that pops up now. Describe that mood and make a gesture capturing how you behave when you are in that mood. When you have written that gesture down, ask yourself what part of you is most troubled by that mood. Let it just pop into your awareness. Make a note about this, too.

The next step is exciting. Let's find out the "direction" the earth gives you for the mood and for the part of you that opposes that direction and use them in a "vector walking" process. Mark a place to start from on the ground with the piece of paper having the plus sign. (By the way, if you can't stand or walk, you can mark the starting point on paper and do the entire vector-walking process on paper.) Recall and feel your worst mood and make a face that goes with it. Then ask the earth to turn you in a direction that you intuitively feel is associated with that mood. (Or feel and draw a line on paper showing this direction.) Take a few steps in the direction of that mood; your body will know how many steps are right.

From the end point of that "mood vector," now remember the part of you that is most disturbed by this mood and feel its energy in your body. Make a face that goes with it. Then let the earth turn you in the direction associated with that part of yourself and take a few steps in that direction. Your body will know how many. Mark your ending point on the ground with the piece of paper having the star sign.

Now let's add these two "mood vectors" together. As separate vectors, they form a zigzag path. To add them, think of how a bird could simply fly from the beginning (+) to the end point (*). Let's find that bird's flight path. Go back to the starting point (+) and slowly move directly to the end point (*). Once you have found this vector, walk along it from point (+) to point (*) a couple of times, sentiently and slowly. As you walk, catch any tiny sensations, feelings, or images that pop up. While walking, you may sense the meaning of that bird's flight path. Let's call this path the "big U."

Now walk along this U again and sense its presence, its atmosphere. If you can sense the significance of this direction, describe it in words. Feel this "big U" path and make some motions or sounds that go with it.

When you are ready, associate those feelings and motions or sounds with a piece of land. This spot may be the same as or different from the signature field you identified in exercise 6a. Imagine standing on that land. Feel the atmosphere and field there and notice their effect on your body. Let that place make a sound and begin to dance you. When you are ready, make a quick sketch on the collage page in square #6b to remind you of this dance and energy. Name it with a couple of words. This atmosphere is an aspect of your signature field and is probably similar to the one you found in #6a.

Now while you are on this aspect of your signature field, let your processmind experience and deal with your worst mood. Remember that worst mood. Your processmind's signature field will know how to deal with it. This may be a very noncognitive process. Be sure to make notes about your insights, vectors, and experiences on the collage pages in square #6b.

For example, my worst mood happened after having the flu months ago. I was tired out, and the part of me that was most disturbed by that depleted state was my energetic self, my normal vibrant energy. The bad mood vector went straight north, and the vector for the energetic part of me most disturbed by that mood went east, toward the East Coast where I grew up; you have to be tough to survive there. However, when I walked from (+) to (*) along the U vector and felt the presence of that big U experience, I found myself in my signature field, the Oregon coast. It was nighttime, and I could feel the place's power dancing me. My experience was wavelike. How did my processmind signature field and big U experience deal with my fatigue?

As the Oregon coast, I could feel how the sea rises and falls, how it has energy and then is quiet. The processmind is neither high nor low, energetic or tired; it simply flows from high tide to low tide in a natural meditative rhythm. The sea is quiet and then suddenly springs up with energy. I realized that both my fatigue and my energy are part of a unified flow. There is no "bad" mood. It is simply part of a larger picture with which I was not in touch. The vector of the bad mood plus the vector of energy formed the big U direction, which was associated with the processmind's signature field (see figure 6.4).

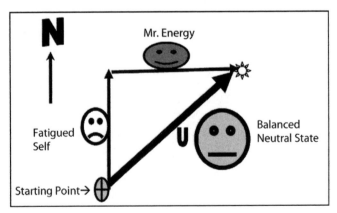

Figure 6.4. Dynamic of Arny's Processmind Signature Field. My bad mood (fatigued self) went north; the "Mr. Energy" part of me went east; walking the U vector resulted in the neutral state of processmind.

Perhaps you noticed that your worst mood is actually part of the processmind's nature. A problem is just an aspect of the processmind trying to reach awareness. What your everyday self experiences as a problem may be needed to "balance" you. The processmind experience expresses itself in part through the diversity of your phases and feelings. Your signature field, your earth spot, has the ability to deal with, encompass, and "under-stand" anything you experience.

We now have two different ways to get to your deepest self. You can dive in directly and meditate to identify with the signature field of your earth spot, as in exercise 6a. Alternatively, you can begin with your worst mood, add it to the aspect of you disturbed by it, and arrive at your deepest self, as in exercise 6b. Which method you use depends upon what you are feeling in a given moment. They are equally powerful routes to your processmind. Having no problems is no better or worse than having some. Knowing this could be an experience of kensho!

THINGS TO THINK ABOUT

1. You feel "under-stood" when you are in contact with your processmind's earth-based signature field.
2. Pointing to the earth was part of the Buddha's enlightenment process.
3. Your worst mood or problem, from the processmind's viewpoint, is only one phase or part of itself.

THE GROUND OF BEING AND SATORI IN RELATIONSHIPS

It was stormy weather on the Oregon coast when Amy and I began to speak at a large seminar we were giving there on the topic of relationships. The following were the first sentences of my introduction:

> There are huge winds today on the coast. I can hear the roar of the wind as it sails through the trees. With the rain pouring down and the high winds blasting our tin roof overhead, I can hardly hear myself speak. Perhaps Mother Nature wants to speak. Why is she so wild today? Or rather, why I am so quiet and observing her to be the one so wild? I wish she were quieter so I would not have to raise my voice. Hmmm . . . relationships . . . I love them, and they sometimes make me wild!
>
> The wind brings me closer to my excitement about the topic of relationships. (*The wind outside quiets down.*) What is relationship? If it is with a lover, we call it a love process. With a business contact, it is a business relationship. With an enemy, it is a battle. However, regardless of how you name a relationship, regardless of how the content and themes vary, the essence or dreamlike processmind field that brings people together seems to remain the same.
>
> In consensus reality, relationship is about two or more people; it is about issues, awareness of facts, and visible signals, and it is about dreams and dreaming—signals you make but do not identify with.

But at the deepest essence level, relationship is about an almost non-verbal experience, a field with a mind of its own, a processmind.

In the preceding chapters, I have focused mainly upon the individual, showing ways a person can get in touch with her or his deepest self as it is connected to the earth. With this chapter I turn to the processmind or field with regard to relationships.

THE ROSHI'S PROCESSMIND

To understand how each relationship has its own special field, let's begin with an example. Amy told me the following story about our friend Keido Fukushima, a Zen roshi and the head abbot of the Rinzai Zen sect. He lives today at Tofukuji Monastery in Kyoto, Japan. You can also find this story in his biography.[1]

During his training, the Roshi had two teachers, one very severe and the other very gentle. One day while he was sitting with his severe master, the Roshi spoke about the gentle Zen master. The severe Zen master asked, "How do you like the gentle one?" The Roshi replied, "That gentle one makes me feel really peaceful." Then, pointing to the strict teacher in front of him, he added, "You make me nervous!" At this point, both the Roshi and his stern Zen master laughed so hard, they almost fell to the floor! Their shared Zen minds, the Buddha-based nature of their relationship, allowed them to appreciate their diversity and even joke about it.

This story has two messages for me. The first is that there is no single kind of Zen mind. Some Zen or processminds are sweet and gentle, whereas others are wild and severe. The second message is that accessing your processmind allows you to be open and honest with people near you. Many people would simply be polite and not tell a respected teacher that he or she is severe. But with your processmind, you can say and do almost anything, because "nothing" (i.e., the field) is doing it. This is the main point I want to make in this chapter: to enjoy and be more fluid in relationships, to find your own processmind and/or the processmind of the relationship.

FOCUS ON THE RELATIONSHIP'S FIELD

The relationship's field is also a key to healing relationship problems. In *The Shaman's Body*, I wrote about how African healer-shamans work with couples. When a couple came to them with relationship problems, the shamans would "feel" the situation, wait until they knew what to do, and then send the people home. Later when the shamans invited the couples back, the relationships were always better. The shamans were working with the processmind field of the relationship and therefore did not need to focus on the relationship's parts or the individuals, even though they were very cordial to them. Just meditating on the relationship's field, on its presence and deepest part, was enough.

I remember working on a relationship situation at the end of the 1960s consisting of five people who lived together. Their relationship was a kind of "group-bed-ship" scene. I was just beginning my practice and did not yet know what I was doing. I was unable to facilitate their interpersonal conversation. What a mess! They yelled at each other in such a way that I could not identify the problem. Eventually, one of them said that the only good thing about their "scene" was their huge futon—it was very big and soft. Then there was a pause. In that moment I realized what they were saying: the only thing they really shared was their bedroom experiences. Finally, I made my first successful intervention. With a bit of encouragement from me, they all began to speak about the nature of that futon! For a few minutes, they themselves became "softer" and happier. We discussed futons in the greatest imaginable detail.

At the time, I could not figure out why everyone was suddenly happier, but now I know. Their futon symbolized the processmind of their relationship. Being tough was their everyday, primary group process, and their futon gave them a rest from it—temporarily. If they were consulting me today, I would suggest that they recall that futon (or its earth-based association) and feel it while speaking together.

The Deep Democracy of Relationships

Democracy suggests that all people are equal and should have equal representation. My definition of deep democracy in the *Leader as Martial Artist* extends the idea of democracy by saying that all levels of consciousness are also of equal value and should also have equal representation. I speak especially about three levels of consciousness: consensus reality, dreamland, and the essence level. In consensus reality, relationships are about the two or more people involved, their words and their issues. In the dreamland aspect of the relationship—in the often-marginalized subjective connection between people—you find their body signals and their dreams. At the essence level of the relationship, there is the processmind field. That field is the relationship's true home, its "Buddha nature," the individuals' common ground.

How do you recognize that field? By what you hear, feel, or see the people sharing. For example, if you are jogging on the beach and come across a couple sitting and looking at the sea, in that moment, the sea is what they share. Knowing this allows you to speak with them even without knowing them. If you gently catch their attention by speaking about the sea as if to the common ground for their relationship, they will probably feel like chatting about the sea as well. Talk to the field between the people. When you do, they will probably feel not invaded but joined.

The relationship's processmind field is not just a shared event but a presence living within and around the relationship. In a way, a relationship is a nonlocal field seeking to show itself. It holds the subtle power and metaskill to deal with the relationship situation. This is because communication between people is composed of signals and fields.

Let me explain. In figure 7.1, the horizontal arrows represent the signals we send and the feedback we get from others. With the help of a video camera, you can identify the physical origins of these signals, the

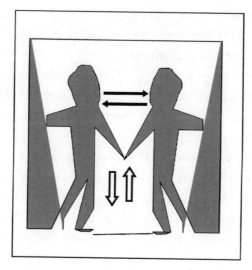

Figure 7.1. Causal and Entangled
Relationship Signals and Field.

voices and gestures. One person might say, for example, "I said this!" The other person might respond with, "No, you said that!" At this level the exchange is local, body-oriented, and causal—one signal in one person gives rise to a reaction in the other. However, much of what happens between people cannot be seen with a video camera and is not only causal. I call these dreamlike communications "entangled" because of their similarity to quantum theory. They are nonlocal and arise in several places at once without any visible local body signal. In the figure, these nonlocal entangled signals are represented as vertical arrows going upward and downward between the two people.

ACTION AT A DISTANCE: ENTANGLEMENT IN RELATIONSHIPS

We human beings (and possibly everything else in the universe) connect from a given locality—that is, from and through our body locations—

and also nonlocally through entanglement. In physics, "entanglement" refers to the way particles or molecules that arise from the same source or are part of the same quantum system connect with one another without any visible signal exchange. How? No one has the final answer to this question. Scientists simply speak of "action at a distance," to use a phrase from physics. (I explain more about quantum entanglement in chapter 15.)

As a psychologist, I use the idea of entanglement to view people as parts of psychological systems—relationships or feeling connections—and in those systems as behaving like quantum objects. If we feel connected to others, some of our experiences and signals connect regardless of how far apart we are from one another. In the quantum world, in principle, parts of quantum systems remain connected even if they are at the opposite ends of the universe.[2]

There is certainly much anecdotal evidence about this nonlocal connection between people. With the help of telephones and email, many people today have the experience of thinking of someone and then suddenly hearing from them. However, here I am mainly concerned with the practical aspects of entanglement. For example, some signals are reactive and caused, whereas other signals seem to be "entangled" as if they were expressions coming from the field between the two people. One possible effect is ambiguity about who did what first or second. Each partner may feel, "I did this because you did that," but when they try, they find it impossible to tell who did what first!

Entanglement also occurs with objects. We often say, "Such-and-such caught my attention," as if the object *made* us observe it. In previous work I have spoken of this experience as "quantum flirts." The words move out of metaphor and into possibility when we consider the presence of a "shared field" encompassing you and the things that spontaneously catch your attention, entangling the observer and observed. Though we think we observed something, perhaps it did indeed "catch" our attention; perhaps the field itself is showing itself in terms of the observer and the observed.

To see what I mean, try the following innerwork exercise: When you are ready, close your eyes and relax. Then let your eyes open again on their own, and when they do, with half-open eyes gaze around the space where you are right now. Let some one thing catch your attention. If you don't know which thing, let your unconscious mind choose. Look at that object, see it, and imagine becoming it. Can you sense that what you are looking at is somehow part of who you are? What do you share with whatever caught your attention? In what sense is this shared thing *in* you but also all *around* you, or at least *between* you and the thing that caught your attention? In what way is this shared quality an aspect of your own processmind as you may know it from previous exercises?

From the everyday viewpoint, relationships, whether between people and things or just between people, are created by people. But from the essence-level viewpoint, relationships arise in response to a shared "something" without particular locality, a nonlocal field that arises through the diversity of two or more people or a person and an object. This way to look at relationships can yield practical insights. For example, experiment with seeing a friend, a couple, a family, or a large group with which you are engaged as a field trying to show itself or to become aware of itself. You may find that you are less likely to turn against some of your friends or members of a team. If you are a facilitator this is a crucial thought. Instead of thinking, "This is a good or bad part of a group," consider the field between the participants as trying to reach awareness.

THE GROUND OF BEING IN RELATIONSHIPS

To work on relationships between people, start with what the people share and remember it while talking about problems. Allow time for them to speak about their individual experiences of the relationship's signature field. Taking your own relationships as an example, try to talk about a favorite space associated with each relationship. You might ask yourself and your partner or friends, "What relationship spot of ours do you like the most?" Everybody has a favorite relationship locale. Get to know that area and its field. Perhaps this is what mystics mean when they speak of connecting to the "ground of being."

For example, the German-American Christian theologian Paul Tillich said that Christ is "she or he who is no longer alienated from the ground of being." His vision of Christ is as a part of you that is no longer alienated from this highest principle. In this sense the processmind is a "ground" in you or in a relationship. Perhaps Rumi, the thirteenth-century Persian poet, Islamic jurist, and theologian, describes the processmind of a relationship the best:[3]

Out beyond ideas of wrongdoing and right doing, there is a field.
I will meet you there.
When the soul lies down in that grass,
the world is too full to talk about language, ideas,
even the phrase *each other* doesn't make any sense.

Here the processmind is literally described as a "field" where the "soul lies down." As Rumi says, here even the term "*each other* doesn't make any sense."

EXERCISE 7A: THE GROUND OF BEING AROUND US

Choose a relationship on which to focus. This can be a present, past, or a potential future relationship. Identify one of its challenges, problems, or potential problems and make a note of it in #7a on the collage page. What do you, or might you, look like when you are caught in a problem situation with that person? Make a face, a gesture, and a statement to express that look. Make a note about the problem and sketch the face at the top or in a corner of 7a. ☹

Now let's find the relationship's ground of being, or processmind. What room, or even spot in a room, is, or could be, the most characteristic spot of that relationship? Let one room or spot pop up. Depending on how formal, casual, or intimate the relationship is, it might be a place in an office, in your home, at a favorite restaurant, and so on. Now feel that space and get in touch with its nature. What is it like? What are the walls and furnishings made of? What does it smell and feel like? Can you see outside? If so, what do you see? Feel the atmosphere of that room, and when you are ready, let it move you a little bit.

As the atmosphere moves you, try to sense, imagine, or associate an earth spot, real or imaginary, that best corresponds to the atmosphere of that room. It might be the land area where that room is, or it may be elsewhere on earth. Once you know this area, go there in your imagination and feel its presence and power. Let that presence and power move you. That is, shapeshift and become this earth spot, its field and processmind. How is this field characteristic of that relationship? Make a note about this and a quick energy sketch of the field in 7a to remember it later on.

While being that field, let it move or even dance you, whatever that means to you. Use this processmind experience to meditate on that relationship, following your inner experiences. In what sense could this field be the "ground of being" of that relationship, the processmind "field" beyond right and wrong? When you are ready, as your processmind, look back at your normal self, at the face and gestures you made to typify you in the midst of that relationship problem, and give your ordinary self some relationship advice. In the future, you can return to this ground of being when you need to do relationship "housekeeping."

I used this exercise to work on my relationship with Amy. Sometimes she gets into an unhappy state because of what she calls her inner critic, a "demon" that criticizes her. After a while, I too get into a poor mood because I just don't agree with her critic's viewpoint, and I criticize the critic. I used to argue with her inner critic. As you can imagine, that approach rarely helped much!

So how did I change? I found the signature room of our relationship to be the living room in our house at the Oregon coast. From that room you can look out at the sea. Before the house was built, a radar station stood on the land, looking out over the coast. So the energy of looking out over the sea characterizes that room. The view and space and earth there make me feel like sketching the symbol for infinity (see figure 7.2). When I am in that room, on the hillside overlooking the coast, and look back at myself in the midst of problems, my processmind suggests this: Rather than getting caught in the moment, remember and flow with the rising and falling sea, splash in the waves, relate to the spirit of that relationship. Sense the wonders of the shared ground and let the sea do the rest.

When you work alone, just getting to the earth spot associated with the room will be helpful. When working face-to-face with your friend, allow time for each of you to first find the relationship's processmind individually. Each of you will have your own view of that earth spot. The important thing is to remain aware of it while you are with the other person.

Remembering the processmind while you are in relationship calls for being "half in, half out," that is, remaining connected to your pro-

Figure 7.2. Infinity.

cessmind while relating to the everyday reality of yourself and the other person. This is the essence of deep democracy. When you are half in and half out, you are more congruent and will give fewer confusing double signals.

EXERCISE 7B: VECTOR WORK IN RELATIONSHIPS

For those who are interested, here is another approach to the relationship's processmind using the relationship's vectors. This approach reveals more about the relationship's diversity. (You may want to review the "vector walking" material in chapter 6.) You can do this exercise individually or with your friend.

Meditate on your general sense of the earth for a moment. Now mark the starting point of your vector walk with a (+) on the ground. Feel your own being, sense the earth, and let the earth turn you until it shows you the direction in which *you* should move. Take a few steps in that direction; your body will know how many.

From this new point, imagine and feel the other person, and let the earth turn you again to show you *that person's direction.* Take a few steps in that direction and mark your ending point on the ground with an (*). (See figure 7.3.)

Now go back to the beginning point (+) and walk directly and slowly from there to the end point (*). As you walk that U line, notice any tiny sensations, fantasies, or feelings that arise. Catch the meaning of that direction. Walk that path a few times to discover and feel the meaning of this U direction. This entire process can be noncognitive in nature. Just trust your experience.

Walk that "big U" path as many times as you need to feel its meaning. Notice what it tells you about the relationship.

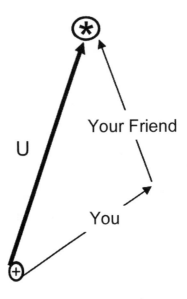

Figure 7.3. U, You, and Friend.

While walking that line, imagine or feel what kind of earth-based place might be associated with it. This could even be the place you are going toward while walking the U line, or it could be another.

Go to that earth spot now in your imagination, and feel it as a field of power and presence. Let it move you. Let it move your hand and make an energy sketch on the collage pages in square #7b. Add a couple of words describing this field. Take time to experience this field, the processmind of the relationship. Notice the difference between this relationship processmind and your everyday self. Let this signature field of the relationship's processmind move/dance you about, and then use that processmind field for a few minutes to follow your own body signals. Make a sketch and notes in section #7b in the collage pages.

When I did this exercise together with Amy, the resultant big U went straight to Kenya. The U line and Kenya were associated in my mind with shamanistic experiences Amy and I had in Kenya many years ago. The land most characteristic of these experiences, however, turned out to be not in Kenya, as I might have expected, but on that Oregon coast hillside again, the place where we now live. Why was the U line associated with the field of the Oregon coast? Perhaps because of the shamanic experiences we have had in this amazing spot. In any case, the infinity symbol appeared again in my sketch, the same as in exercise 7a.

Once you have done this exercise, alone or with your friend, meditate together, remembering your earth-based processmind experiences. They will tell you what to do and when. I suggest first sharing your processmind experiences. Then, while you are each in your own experience of the relationship's signature field, let your processmind follow and flow. Stay with your processmind, being half inside, half outside, while flowing with your own and the other's signals.

If you get distracted, go back to the processmind's signature field of that relationship and let it deal with the distractions, or just continue to notice signals, double signals, and so on. The two of you will know when you are done. Finally, your bodies will know when it's time to discuss things. As you begin to talk in a more or less normal state of consciousness, stay close to your processmind experience. When you are both ready, make a sketch together in #7b that represents what you have experienced. Add a few words to describe it.

The important point about this exercise is that it does not call for much signal awareness because your processmind perceives and facilitates signals before they reach your everyday consciousness. From the viewpoint of your processmind, confusing signals and double signals arise because of fixed identities. It's normal to have a fixed identity in consensus reality, but this identity does not contain the totality of your relationship abilities. Remember the Roshi and his severe teacher almost rolling over because they were laughing so hard. In that moment they no longer self-identified as either student or teacher. In fact, the Roshi, who was the student, in that moment became, as it were, his teacher's teacher. The processmind is free and unpredictable!

What if you have a deep relationship feeling for somebody, but for one reason or another you cannot live it out? Perhaps exterior constraints limit the actualization of the relationship. Of course, there is no single answer to such a question. However, from the processmind's viewpoint, the relationship always exists, regardless of how it is realized in everyday reality. In this sense, you are always in relationship to others, even those you don't like very much! In a way, you can't "do" relationship work; you can only practice relating, that is, being familiar with and then becoming the relationship's field.

THINGS TO THINK ABOUT

1. Relationship is a dreamlike field experience and a consensus reality experience expressed by two or more separate individuals.
2. You don't have to follow words or signals when you are close to the processmind. It follows signals almost before they arise.

CHAPTER 8

TEAMWORK, OR WHY THE
ENEMY IS NEEDED

Just as innerwork is central to relationship work, so relationship work is basic to teamwork. However, we usually forget the processmind when working with teams or large groups. Such work can be as exhilarating as it can be depressing. Teams can be awesome because many minds and bodies together can be more creative than an individual. On the other hand, if the team is in conflict, or if you do not like somebody on it, you find yourself saying, "Oh, if only so-and-so was not on this team. Who needs this team, anyway? I would rather do it myself!"

The processmind is a powerful team and organizational facilitator. In small teams and in large groups up to about one thousand, I have seen it turn even apparent enemies into teammates. In this chapter I focus on the processmind's application to teams of between two and twenty-two people, that is, groups small enough that all the people know one another.

See figure 8.1 below for a description of the processmind as facilitator. At the bottom of the figure is a face representing the processmind. It is a round face in a square area to symbolize the processmind as an ineffable feeling, as well as a dreamland figure and also a real facilitator, a "square" person in everyday reality. As long as your everyday identity, the "you" in the dark box at the top left, is not in contact with your processmind, you usually speak only as a one-sided part in a field with other one-sided parts of your team. You are all just "squares" in consensus reality.

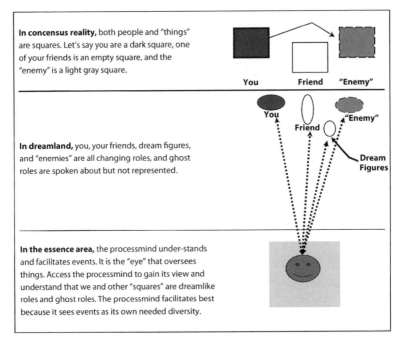

In concensus reality, both people and "things" are squares. Let's say you are a dark square, one of your friends is an empty square, and the "enemy" is a light gray square.

You   Friend   "Enemy"

In dreamland, you, your friends, dream figures, and "enemies" are all changing roles, and ghost roles are spoken about but not represented.

You   Friend   "Enemy"   Dream Figures

In the essence area, the processmind under-stands and facilitates events. It is the "eye" that oversees things. Access the processmind to gain its view and understand that we and other "squares" are dreamlike roles and ghost roles. The processmind facilitates best because it sees events as its own needed diversity.

Figure 8.1. How the Processmind Facilitates.

The square as a symbol means you don't roll and flow. If you dream or fantasize about your team, you can know the members as dreamland "projections" of yourself or as potential team "roles." By realizing that the squares can become round roles and flow, you become a facilitator of the team situation. In addition, if you can connect to the processmind, all the roles and people are seen as momentary aspects of the overall situation and of your largest self. The "ghost roles" mentioned in the figure refer to those people and things (such as the boss or the environment) that group members talk of but do not directly represent.

THE GARDEN'S PROCESSMIND

To understand the team's processmind in a less theoretical way, let's consider Amy and her garden. Amy's garden is visible from a window of our house. When we both look out of our window, most of the time Amy looks at her garden first. It seems to want her to look at it. Frequently she says, "Oh, look at that little carrot." More recently she's been saying, "Look at that squirrel run by . . . oh, that little pest, it wants to eat my garden!" Other garden "enemies" include the deer, the birds, the elk, and the black bears from the nearby national forest.

That squirrel was such a troublemaker that Amy and I discussed the situation. At first my idea that the "enemy is your teammate" made absolutely no sense to her—or to me! But as we worked on the processmind of Amy's garden, we realized that the garden area includes not only the plants and vegetables but all the things around the garden, including the squirrel. The garden is literally the ground underneath us, a true ground of being. It is both a real and an essencelike earth power.

The dream roles in the garden area include Amy the gardener, the squirrel as perceived thief, me, the carrots and peas, and so on. And at the same time, those juicy carrots, the squirrel, Amy, and I are real square members of the "garden team" in everyday reality. At its essence level, the garden's processmind is a kind of totem spirit, which I have positioned beneath Amy and the squirrel in figure 8.2.

When Amy worked on her garden "team" situation, she experienced the garden spirit figures or totem spirits as the organizing intelligence of the garden. She said that the garden field had entangled her and the squirrel in a kind of battle. The more she and I protected the garden against intruders with fencing, the more the squirrel found its way in. And the more it found its way into the garden, the harder we worked. However, from the garden's processmind or totem spirit viewpoint, Amy and the squirrel and the carrots and peas and everything else were an expression of the field's presence and diversity. Amy is the human gardener, and she and I are "eaters," but the squirrel is an eater as well—and a competitor!

Amy and the squirrel were entangled; they "flirted" with one another. Why? We can surmise that it was because of the ground they share. Squirrels don't flirt much with me. Whales catch my attention

Figure 8.2. Black squirrel, Amy, and Garden Spirit.

most often—they "flirt" with me. Why am I more likely to observe whale-spouting flirts while Amy first sees squirrels? Because my totem spirit entangles me closely with the sea, whereas Amy's nature is more entangled by her garden.

In any case, Amy focused on the nature of her garden, found the garden's processmind, and from its viewpoint saw that the vegetables, the squirrels, and Amy are all part of that mind. She immediately knew that the processmind area loved the squirrel. Squirrels gather food, eat it, or store and protect it in their "homes." The garden, too, was squirrel-like; it too wanted to protect its area. With this realization Amy immediately set about creating a better, stronger fence around that garden to store "her" food. To her delight, this fence kept out not only the squirrel but also the deer, elk, and other animals. Better yet, Amy no longer harbored ill feelings toward the squirrel. She even took him as one of her teachers. Her former enemy became a needed teammate. She even made a YouTube film of the squirrel spinning around in circles.

What's the difference between just asking "What have you projected onto the squirrel?" and processmind work? In the former, you remain yourself and "integrate" the other into yourself. In the processmind work, you and the other are both yourselves and expressions of a deeper unity. A team is not only "a number of persons and/or animals associated together in work," as the Merriam-Webster dictionary tells us. That's only part of the definition. A more complete viewpoint sees the team as everything connected with a given land spot, including you, your friends, your enemies, and all the spirits and ghosts of the team's processmind.

THE PROCESSMIND AT WORK

Let me give another example of how processmind makes teammates even out of enemies. In the late 1990s Amy and I were working on a city forum concerning Aboriginal land right issues in a certain city in Australia. A large group of people had gathered to discuss the issues. There was much enmity, a lot of painful facts, and excruciating stories from the past about how the Aboriginal people had suffered from racist policies.

In that large meeting room, the real oppressors and the oppressed were present. But because of the history, there were also many roles and ghost roles represented by different people at different moments.

Near the end of one of the large group processes involving terrible conflict, an Aboriginal man came forward. He seemed to be in an altered state—at least compared to the rest of us, who were angry, depressed, and nervous about the stress and strain of the moment. This man walked quietly forward as if he had been in meditation. In a soft voice he said that he sensed the presence of "Mother Earth" and that he would speak for her now. Then he began to speak as if he were Mother Earth, the processmind itself. In a slow, quiet, and proud voice, he said, "I am here. I am here. And you are here as well. We are all on different sides. But I am here, holding you, and I will hold everything that is here in the present and past. There is room for everyone."

His voice and feelings had a deep effect on people; some even cried. He went on to say, "I will always be here. Even when you are gone I will be here." In that moment, all the people settled down. His words and presence helped everyone become a team, and we all began to work on the future of land rights issues in Australia. He turned enemies into teammates. He was "half in and half out"; he was in touch with the deepest level of that community as well as with the real people. He created the atmosphere in which we could work together, and that atmosphere is the point. It makes working together possible.

TEAMWORK'S DEEP DEMOCRACY

This Australian story reminds me of the totem poles of Native American groups with which we have worked. The many mythic images on the totem pole are viewed as working together. See, for example, the Haida totem pole in figure 8.3. The totem pole is the center of a tribe's community, the guide, and the "voice" of the earth in that place. On any one pole, the various mythic, or dreamland, community roles are represented

Figure 8.3. Haida Totem Pole. A superposition of community roles represented by totem figures.

as totem figures in superposition with one another—that is, though separate, they work together as a unity.

Teams of people do not always cooperate—in fact, more often than not they compete. Enemies are rarely considered teammates! They only become teammates when seen from the processmind's viewpoint. Everyone needs this viewpoint. Just think of all the teams of which you are a part. Think of the people who live near and around you as teammates. There are kitchen teams, city teams, face-to-face teams, virtual teams, people with whom we work over the Internet. In a way, the entire planet is a team because we share at least two common purposes: we must all breathe, and we are all trying to survive. Moreover, we all live on the same planet.

To help a team, begin with your view of them. I think of teams as composed of people, animals, and the environment working together or against one another in conjunction with history, dreams, roles, and ghosts—all of which share a common processmind. In the case of our planet, that common ground is the earth. To identify the (dreamland) roles and ghost roles in a team, listen to the gossip. How do people identify one another according to their jobs and natures? For example, there are bosses, secretaries, janitors, and so on. And, according to the gossip, there are abusers, revolutionaries, addicts, the lazy ones who never complete things, the ones having an affair, the "customer," and so on. Once you know the people, parts, and roles, then find the processmind: It has the most powerful metaskills to help with team and group work.

There are various ways of finding a team's processmind. You can guess at the processmind based on verbal or written statements describing the group's mission or purpose, but this is not enough. You must ponder and get to what you suspect is the essence of that group. For example, General Motors used to say that its mission was "to be the world leader in transportation." But the essence of GM's vision might have been to help people become mobile at all levels: in communication, in thinking, in relationships, in moving from one place to another. The essence of a mission statement is so elemental, it can hardly be stated. Like individuals and like couples, businesses and organizations usually forget the vision and passion that originally brought them together. Whatever specific problems they identify, distance from their vision's essence is a major difficulty. Getting closer to that essence, helping the group connect with its processmind, equips the group to solve its own problems.

Amy and I recently worked for Naropa University. It is a wonderful school and, like all organizations, it had problems. We supported them by reminding them of the spiritual tradition behind the mythic figure of Naropa, the name of the school. Naropa was an Indian Buddhist mystic and monk who was born in 956 and died in 1041. In his late twenties, he decided to spend his life looking for his teacher, Tilopa. He underwent terrible trials to find his teacher. He was robbed, beaten, and hurt in other ways. Finally, when he felt he could go no further, he decided to give up his life. Just before slitting his throat, Tilopa appeared to him as a blue light. The visionary teacher said, "I was present in all your problems. I was behind all that happened, teaching you detachment from your identity." Suddenly Naropa was enlightened, and he went on to become a great teacher.

To make my story short, simply reminding the university people of Naropa and Tilopa and that apparent problems could be teachings about detachment was helpful. They quickly resolved the "problem" they had been facing.

Often the processmind of a group involves a shift to a higher, more global perspective. The Dutch painter Adriaen van de Venne portrays this in *Fishing for Souls*, painted in 1614 (see figure 8.4). The painting is a satirical allegory of the conflict between religious groups in Holland. On the left of this picture are the Catholics and on the right are Protestants. Fishing boats on the wide river are already full of people, with others still being hauled in, naked and nearly drowning. Crowds from each group fill the riverbanks, and there is a rainbow in the background above the river.

Figure 8.4. *Fishing for Souls* by Adriaen van de Venne, 1614, Rijksmuseum, Amsterdam.

From my viewpoint, the river shows the moment-to-moment struggle between the two religions for "lost souls." However, the incredible overarching rainbow seems ready to unify all the discordant parts in the painting. The rainbow is in another space, a psychological "hyperspace" or "higher" dimension, and it functions as a presence and a signature field image.

Figure 8.5 illustrates the nature of hyperspace. On the left, you see everyday reality represented as a flatland, a two-dimensional surface, like a flat piece of paper. Imagine that flatland occupied by two-dimensional flatheads! A line drawn on the land becomes a barrier. To reach each other, the flatlanders need to access a third dimension. Once the height dimension is added, they can get over the barrier, as in the right-hand illustration.

The processmind's essence level and dreamland are like height, like the rainbow—bridging our polarizations in everyday reality. We want to find that "rainbow," the spirit of the earth, the processmind surrounding organizations.

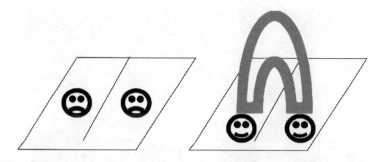

Figure 8.5. Hyperspace. The two people on the left can't get along until, on the right, we add a third dimension, a processmind "hyperspace."

YOUR FAMILY TOTEM

Let's warm up for the team development exercise that follows by finding the processmind of one of the most difficult organizations imaginable: your family or caretaking system! Think about your family system for a moment. What is of interest here is not the moods of your family members, not the good and bad things they did, but the essence of your family system. What motivated that system? What were its core strivings?

Even if that family group is now fragmented or has all sorts of problems, ask yourself: what power or field might symbolize its essence? You can find that answer in many ways, but to begin with you can consider: Where did your family members come from, your grandparents and great-grandparents? What did they suffer? At what did they succeed? What did they long for? Think of their deep background motivation. Were they city people? Were they slaves? Were they migrants seeking liberty? With what part of what country are they now associated?

What earth spot might you associate with the essence of your family system? If you find it, jot it down and remember it when you have to deal with family members about difficult issues. Try to hold onto that image when you are with them—be half in, half out.

For example, for me, the Statue of Liberty represents my family system. They were immigrants seeking freedom. When I was a little boy,

Figure 8.6. The Statue of Liberty as a Totem Earth Spot.

my mother took me to see the Statue of Liberty. At that time, I was not interested in that cold, windy place by the sea. But for my parents, freedom, liberty, and hope were huge issues. I know that this statue is not a symbol of freedom for everyone, yet it is for me. My mother said, and my grandmother reiterated, that this statue allowed us to be free. When I deal with potentially stressful family matters, I think of that statue, I remember liberty, and things go well.

EXERCISE 8: KENSHO IN TEAMWORK

Now let us turn to organizations or teams with which you are working. Choose one such team, family, or group system you want to work with in a better way. Recall the toughest person or worst situation in that team's experience and note it in #8 in the collage pages. Then relax, drop that troublesome situation from your mind for the time being, and recall instead the team's most characteristic atmosphere. Let your creative mind sense and imagine it, and then quickly sketch a field representing this atmosphere around that team. Let that field move your hands; also make a few motions and sounds to represent it.

When you are ready, breathe into that atmosphere to get to its essence. Let the earth itself reveal an earth spot that might represent the atmosphere, or field, of this team. Once a place comes to mind, go there in your imagination. Notice and feel the earth's presence and the spirit of that area. Let that presence and energy move you to make gestures. Make a quick energy sketch of that place on the square on the collage page and name it.

When you are ready, let go of your identity as a person for a moment and become the land itself. Be that spot for a minute or two. What is it like for you to be the processmind and signature field of that group? Just notice whatever comes up. Be the spirit of that land, its mind, and just follow its awareness in meditation. Let it move you and make sounds or songs through you for a couple of minutes.

While being that spot, think about that troublesome group situation—the people, the systems. Being in your processmind might enable you to "know" something that might be helpful for everyone. What is the land's advice? Imagine how this process-mind would deal with the most difficult person on that team or the most difficult situation that team faces.

Now in your imagination, staying half in, half out, imagine the processes that might emerge as you follow the flow of events and signals. How can this earth spot help the team's situation? Imagine actualizing this advice—that is, imagine being this earth experience and simultaneously bringing it into the team scenario about which you are thinking. How would you be the same as you are normally in that group? How would you be different? Make a note about your experiences in #8 on the collage pages in Appendix B.

CHAPTER 8

One of my students, an instructor at the Process Work Institute
(PWI) in Portland, reported the following:

> What a team! A most interesting issue occurred a few years ago when
> tension temporarily arose between those who were nervous about
> the technical nature of the evolving institute and the more didactic
> people, who were hoping to renew the institute's programs. These two
> roles—I will call them the "dreamers" and the "realists"—after dis-
> agreeing with one another, eventually came together. I followed your
> exercise and felt the characteristically good atmosphere of the insti-
> tute. It was like a kind of humming and a staccato tapping. A swirl-
> ing energy line with linear sections emerged [see the top of figure 8.7
> below]. It was an intelligent and organizing energy. It made a kind of
> "step, step, flow" image.
>
> I associated this energy sketch with the Portland land area where
> the institute is located. I saw a kind of map with square city streets, the
> institute on Hoyt Avenue, and two rivers, the Columbia and the Wil-
> lamette, which flow together in Portland. When I felt that land, I found
> myself humming like the dreamers and then being more linear like the
> realists! I started to swing and dance, I was both straight and fluid, like
> the diagram. That earth-based experience gave me the *feeling about
> the team's processmind; it was both reasonable and clear about making
> steps, and then it could just let go like the rivers.* In that half in, half out
> state, I realized that those rivers come together by themselves. And that
> is what happened! *After a brief debate that I tried to facilitate with my
> processmind, the two sides came together almost magically.*

I did not have to do anything to help this student; his processmind
did what was needed by showing him its appreciation of the earth and
all its people, parts, and rivers. Together with that student's presence, the
group made a transition that eventually satisfied everyone. During one
decisive meeting he supported the dreamers and the more linear think-
ers, one after the other, until they flowed together almost by themselves.

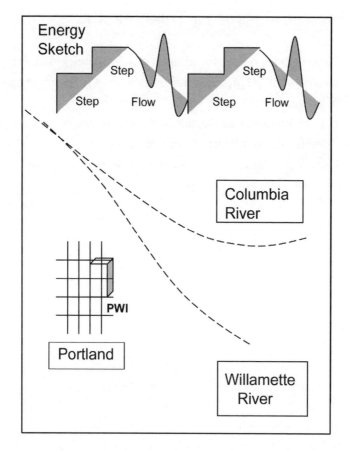

Figure 8.7. The Process Work Institute's Earth Spot.

When you and some of your teammates are ready, each one should sense the atmosphere, or essence, of the group's mission statement, find the organization's processmind, and while staying half in, half out, take your group to the next step. Meditate and be your group's processmind.

I have often noticed then when a whole group meditates on its processmind and uses it during face-to-face interactions, such an intense and lively atmosphere is created that the group often prefers not to break up! That is a good sign, because the team's "ground of being" is a kind of home. And home is a glimpse of enlightenment—kensho in teamwork.

THINGS TO THINK ABOUT

1. From the viewpoint of consensus reality, enemies exist. From the viewpoint of the processmind, everyone is a necessary expression of the same earth spot.
2. Use the processmind during conflict times to enable flatlanders to bridge apparently irreconcilable opposites.
3. Use the processmind to create more sustainable societies.

WORLD WAR, DEATH, AND WORLD TASKS

Seeing one's enemies as potential teammates is a radical concept for the world at large. Recently on a map of the world showing military conflicts as of 2009, I counted nearly thirty dark spots indicating the locations of major wars on our planet. According to the United Nations, a "major war" is a military conflict that inflicts at least one thousand battlefield deaths per year.[1]

These locations form a war strip that goes right around the middle of our planet. But war, in my thinking, is not limited to these places. In many ways, war in one spot means conflict everywhere. All of us participate in war. Think of yourself and others who may not be in a war zone but see pictures of war on the daily news. Some support war, whereas others are warring with those making war. In this way, even a small war is a global event involving all those observers reading the newspapers or the Internet coverage, thinking that one side or both sides are crazy. Some think, "Those people are idiots—why can't they just get along?" Others think that war is due to our evolutionary history. Some think people are inherently violent. Many say we are too ambitious, we have too much "ego." Many suggest that we should "listen to the other" or "turn the other cheek." Since war is so persistent and pervasive, it is important to ask if it serves some larger purpose. Perhaps in addition to all the other reasons for war, something in us is "dying" for war and death, even longing for it. Why? War not only defines the diversity of a given situation by polarizing it, it also hints at death and the possibility of detaching from our everyday minds and roles.

Most of us are attached to our identity: We are this age and this gender, sexual orientation, nationality, race, religion, class, and so on. When we go to sleep at night, we may dream about "the other" as a counterbalance to loosen the grip of this identification and become more fluid. We may dream of attackers not only to express polar opposites within us, but also to "kill" our identity. Similarly, perhaps we are smitten with a longing for war and for death, in part to relax our passionate attachment to our everyday identity.

But let me clarify my position. I do not want anyone to let go entirely of their position, their identity. No. That has never worked. We need to take a stand, define our position, and protect ourselves. However, we can't protect ourselves in a sustainable manner without cognizance of the other, without getting to the essence of the other's position. The easiest way to do this is by using the processmind, because all parties are parts of our deepest processmind. When we drop out of the conflict, at least for a moment and perceive from the processmind's viewpoint, we can identify at least temporarily with first one side, then the other. In other words, our rigid identity "dies" and we move fluidly among identities.

This process is different than total detachment, which can separate us from both our own problems and the problems of others. Accessing the processmind is also more encompassing than the injunction "Love thine enemy." Remember Amy's garden in the previous chapter? By identifying with her deepest self, the processmind, Amy was temporarily the garden, and in that garden there was room for a diversity of beings. In this way, war is neither bad nor good but rather the beginning of a potential relationship process that can go beyond peacefulness into the realm of flow. In contrast, "Love thy enemy" marginalizes the separations of consensus reality and the tendency to protect oneself and fight. My suggestion is to fight when you sense a conflict, allow polarization temporarily to occur, and when the fighting becomes dangerous or impossible, "drop your-self" long enough to find the processmind, which understands and can move between the various positions, which are parts of it.

The possibility of being simultaneously inside and outside a conflict first occurred to me when studying Richard Feynman's description of events in the world of quantum physics. (See my interpretation of this Nobel Prize–winning quantum physicist's work in my *Quantum Mind*.)[2] Feynman spoke about what happens when a piece of matter, such as an electron, enters into an electromagnetic field that can push it about. According to his analysis, one of two scenarios occurs. Only the first one, however, has been seen in the laboratory.

In the first, proven scenario, represented in figure 9.1 by the straight lines, a particle of matter enters a field on the left and moves diagonally upward, that is, forward in time. Simultaneously, a pair of matter/anti-matter particles is created (see bottom right in fig. 9.1). The antimatter particle travels upward left; when it meets the original particle, the two temporarily annihilate each other. Then the new particle created as the antimatter counterpart goes on its way, but it leaves the field in a different direction from that of the original particle. In the second scenario, how-ever, there is only one particle that moves forward and then backward in time, as shown by the snakelike, dashed line with elements of timeless-ness in its open spaces. Now there is no annihilation; the movement of the original particle remains continuous. Feynman likened this second scenario to the view of a pilot in a low-flying plane. Unlike someone on the ground, who sees what looks like two roads on the nearby hills, the pilot from his higher perspective sees not two roads but rather one con-tinuous road with curves in it.

One reason why the second scenario has never been seen in the labo-ratory—and why Feynman and other physicists have not thought further about it—is because at one point that dashed, curved line swings back-ward in time. Only forward movements (the straight lines) toward anni-hilation are perceived in today's physics. However, because the dashed, curving path belongs to the same equations that give rise to the path of

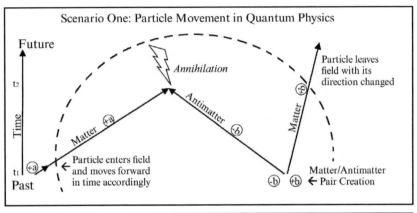

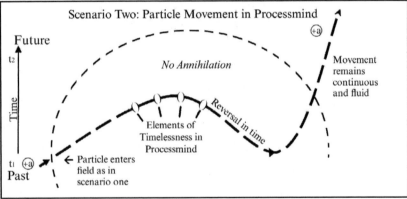

Figure 9.1. The Path of Annihilation versus the Path of Stability, as adapted from Richard Feynman's diagrams. The motion of a particle in time (+a) is toward annihilation as it meets its opposite (-b); conversely, the motion of a particle in processmind moves variably forward and backward in time, not meeting its opposite, and so remains stable.

the arrows, it is part of the overall pattern. It seems to me that the curved line is a metaphor for the timeless nature of the processmind. On this path, instead of creation and annihilation due to our identity as forward movers in time, there is a continuous flow in and out of time.

The point of this book, reiterated here in terms of quantum electrodynamics and war theory, is that we need more access to our processmind's "hyperspaces" outside of everyday time and space. Then, from the viewpoint of that altered state, our own path and the essence of the enemy's path both belong to one continuous, processmind flow. But to find the processmind, you have to let go of your identity as a human being who lives and dies in time. Bring the processmind into conflict work, and amazing things can happen, as we have already seen. Remember the Aboriginal man who spoke for the earth? Remember Amy's garden? Step into and then out of the war zone, and connect to the earth! To change our tendency to war, each of us must model a new world and the ability to access the processmind.

The persistence of war as the world currently practices it—meaning a battle between two or more sides involving land, power, rank, history, economics, religion, and so on—is due in part to denial of the processmind altered state of consciousness and the mythic earth. From the consensus reality viewpoint, war is a conflict between sides that are frozen in their identities and proceeding forward in time toward annihilation. From the processmind viewpoint, war is not only a persistent, frozen state; it is also a process flowing forward and backward in time—or its psychological equivalent, which is being yourself and then, through feeling the earth, reversing your viewpoint to pick up the other's energy.

To get to this viewpoint, take six steps: (1) notice a conflict, (2) go to "war" over it, (3) realize the potential for death, (4) drop into the processmind's hyperspace, and (5) with this altered state of consciousness and new perspective, re-enter conflict between what appeared to be inextricably entangled opposites. (6) Go further and ask the processmind what your world task is. Does this sound too far out? It is! Stay with me. I will make it more realizable by examining ancient shamanic ideas.

THE DEAD AS ROLES IN THE PROCESS

Every day we hear about how many soldiers and civilians were killed in battle in various parts of the world. The dead are spoken about in the news all the time. Thus the dead are real and are also roles in group processes, as are living people, trees, gardens, money, and so on. However, unlike objects and living people, the dead have no one to represent them directly. Thus they are "ghost roles." Since dying can be viewed as leaving your everyday polarized position in order to find the processmind, we need to explore the dying process and represent the dead as "ghost roles." Death is a core issue in war and in life as a whole.

According to the Yaqui Indian sorcerer tradition and other Native American traditions, getting to your "last dance," your mythic essence, is the only thing that can forestall death.[3] The last dance is a warrior's expression of her or his basic self, the processmind dance. I have seen how getting into your deepest self actually makes death irrelevant. Getting into your deepest self and letting it move you at least gives you a sense of wellness.[4]

To move into and beyond war, let's explore the processmind, death, and the last dance in exercise 9. Many people experience body symptoms just when they are facing conflicts, whether inner or outer. Therefore, we will first ponder a symptom that bothers you. Then we are going to use it to work on conflict. How? We are going imagine that it might kill you rapidly. The point is the freedom you might experience from your everyday self that comes from the fear of death. I don't want you to linger in the dying fantasy, but in the experience of freedom from your everyday body and self. You will need to trust your awareness and the integrity of your own experience. At a given moment you will have the chance to relax and "die" and then track the experiences of what happens to you "after death." I will ask: Does your spirit go out of your body? Use your awareness and find out what happens to your presence after death.

EXERCISE 9: CONFLICT, DEATH, AND YOUR WORLD TASK

This exercise begins with considering three general questions. Use #9 on the collage pages in appendix B to jot down your answers. First, choose a conflict in which you are engaged at present, even if it is only a minor one. Make a note identifying the two or more sides involved in this conflict. Second, consider your work. What work are you doing these days? And what do you think your larger world task, or major task in life, might be? After noting down your answers to these questions, ask yourself the third: What is the most troubling or dangerous body symptom you have or fear that you might have (even if it is only a small symptom, but only if there is a little fear associated with it). Note this down, too.

Death Fantasy. When you are ready, imagine having lived well and *very rapidly* dying from that symptom. Remember, this is *just* a fantasy. Do it quickly—don't focus on or worry about the dying process, but simply imagine dying quickly. Let go, relax, lie back, and use your best awareness to track, unfold, and remember your experiences so you can write them down later. Pretend, if you can, that you leave your body as a spirit field or smoky apparition. Do you come out of the body, dissolve in the air or earth, have a form, travel somewhere in the universe? What happens to you as a spirit or field? Take note of these experiences and write them down later in #9 on the collage pages.

One of my students worked with herself on this exercise before helping to facilitate a conflict in Africa. She reported:

> I have huge, business-oriented conflict problems. I see myself dying one day, apparently of fatigue, of old age. I imagine myself getting tired and drifting out of my body. And then what happens? I leave, I go into space and . . . suddenly become aware of an intense desire to want people and planets to dance more together! This sounds strange, but in this state it is real for me.

Totem Field Spirit. Now shape-shift by acting like or becoming this experience or spirit. Sense its movement and presence, if possible. Then imagine what piece of the planet earth might possibly be associated with this after-life spirit. Which spot on the earth most closely represents your presence? See and feel this piece of earth, sense and become its nature in movement. Then imagine what totem animal or imaginary intelligent mythic form or human figure might represent this piece of earth. Sketch the energy of this figure.

Once you know this earth-based totem spirit's energy, imagine being this spirit and let it dance and be you. Draw or sketch this processmind totem experience on the collage pages under #9, and add some notes. While still sensing this earth-based totem spirit, remember the symptom you thought about in the beginning and, as this spirit, explain the meaning or fear of that symptom. Remember yourself as that living human being worrying about her or his symptoms, and as your processmind earth-based field spirit, interact with that person. Make notes about that.

My student went on with her experience:

> I let go, lay back, and suddenly had the fantasy or sense of a spirit leaving my body and flying around in the universe. The intense desire to get people and planets to dance more came back as I encircled the earth. This spirit's freedom to follow what was happening could be represented on earth as the globe itself, pulling all its parts and people together. A mythic global female figure representing this feeling . . . a Pachamama, emerged from the earth, telling me to believe in her and relax more! I realized my fears of old age and death were trying to relax me!

World Task. While still imagining and/or dancing your earth-based spirit field, ask, "If this spirit could incarnate in the form of a real person, what kind of person would that be?" Describe that person on the collage page. Shape-shift and feel or become this person a bit and ask: if you were totally free to be this person, and had no edges or barriers, what would you do in your present life? Make notes.

Now, as your earth-based processmind spirit, look at your everyday self and give her or him a specific world task. This could be the same task that you are already doing, or it could be a new job. How close is the new processmind world task to your present work? What's the difference in content? What's the difference in the way of doing the task?

Finally, as your processmind totem spirit, consider the conflict you identified in the beginning of this exercise. Look at the two or more sides that are in conflict. When you are ready, your processmind spirit may give you a tip about what to do there. Make a note of this.

My student commented:

> I noticed Pachamama . . . she made me cry. She gave me the task of modeling her in everyday life. I realized that modeling the belief and care for all sides and not expecting or trying to get others to do so was how I needed to go further with the conflict work in business in Africa. I realized that to be such a model, I had to swing between conflicting parties at work. Several weeks later, I tried doing that and it went well. . . . By moving more deeply into the altered state of that earth-based Pachamama, I seem to have had a strange effect on making myself and other people feel more relaxed. Parties that had never wanted even to come together to talk decided to try!

WHO ARE YOU?

From consensus reality's viewpoint, you are just a macroscopic Newtonian object, with a certain age and size, weight, chemistry, etc. You were born and will surely die as time moves forward. This viewpoint that you, and others, are only "real" persons moving forward in time is incomplete. Its one-sidedness helps to create the frozen polarities that are basic to war and the fear of death.

From the viewpoint of the processmind you are multidimensional. Yes, you are a "real" person who will one day die, yet simultaneously you are a timeless flow, a totem spirit, that is free of your momentary identity. Identification with this timeless dimension may not only be good for your body, it may also explain recent dreams and allow you to resolve conflicts and be helpful to others, perhaps to the whole world.

Understanding conflict situations as an opportunity to "die," in the positive sense of becoming your processmind's totem spirit in action, can only help you and the rest of our conflicted planet. My interest is not in changing how the world is but rather in taking conflict as a reminder: Find your processmind and the path beyond creation and annihilation. When people do this, large conflicts end sooner and lead to more meaningful creativity.

THINGS TO THINK ABOUT

1. Don't just go to war with war.
2. War signals the need for processmind awareness.
3. Take conflict situations and body fears as opportunities to "die" and find your world task.
4. "Die" before you are killed and bring your totem spirit to life.
5. The ghosts and perhaps solutions to war are the dead, that is, the state of mind we usually associate with death.

CHAPTER 10

THE CITY'S PROCESSMIND: NEW ORLEANS

I n this chapter I want to show how the processmind approach to addressing conflict can be applied in other socially and psychologically traumatic contexts, such as the aftermath of a natural disaster or other catastrophe. For this purpose I will focus on the work Amy and I did in New Orleans after the partial devastation of the city in late August, 2005, in the wake of Hurricane Katrina.

Amy and I had decided to help New Orleans rebuild itself. We were devastated ourselves to learn, a year after the catastrophe, about the rising suicide rate and escalating poverty problems. Few people realized that more than 1,800 people died because of the flooding. That is more than half the number of U.S. soldiers who had died in the Iraq war at that time. Yet there was much less public interest in New Orleans than in the Iraq war, perhaps partly because nature, not a human enemy, was the "problem."

On the one hand, no one could be blamed for the natural catastrophe. On the other hand, everyone blamed everyone else for everything else. Most felt that the catastrophe had been amplified by racism, classism, and the city's incompetence. Many accused the federal government and U.S. president of neglect. The Army Corps of Engineers (who built the inadequate levees) could have done better. Some even complained about God, who was "punishing the people" for various reasons (according to New Orleans's mayor at that time, Ray Nagin).

One thing seemed certain. Everyone and everything connected to that city had been affected. Widespread agony ignites hidden anger and unresolved historical issues. During our time focusing on the city, it often seemed as if no one was able to get along with anyone else. Even organizations who were in New Orleans in the name of helping seemed like battlefields looking for enemies. As soon as we began to organize a forum to help folks there communicate better with one another, other helping groups got into conflict with us. Some told us what not to do, others told us what we should do. Some invited us but then told us not to come. "You will be responsible for everyone's health," they warned, "if another catastrophe occurs during your work here and if people from outside the city are caught in the city and can't get out."

Everyone—including Amy and me—was suffering. Some people suffered from problems I had not dealt with before, such as "water trauma": people were afraid to turn on their showers because of traumatic memories of rain pouring down on them. Trauma influences all kinds of human interactions: relationships, friendships, family situations, connections to the environment, and so on. Institutional neglect and racism are traumatic. Before Hurricane Katrina, two-thirds of New Orleans was African-American; two years later, one half.

What happened to New Orleans is likely to happen to other world cities located on the seacoasts and rivers as the earth moves into the era of global warming. We need to think as scientists, ecologists, and engineers about how to prevent eco-trauma, that is, the disastrous effects of ecological catastrophes upon people and the environment. We also need to think as therapists, coaches, and conflict-resolution facilitators about how to better deal with trauma and intervene in traumatized organizational and city processes.

However, the spirit of cities is powerful, and New Orleans is no exception. As one of the oldest cities in the United States, its nature shows itself in its multicultural heritage, cuisine, architecture, and identity as the birthplace of jazz. Its Mardi Gras celebrations are world famous, as are its French Quarter and Bourbon Street (see figure 10.1).

Figure 10.1. Bourbon Street, New Orleans:
Looking toward Canal Street, 2003.

John Scott, an African-American artist, said of New Orleans, "There is so much history and cultural richness in that city that it oozes up out of the sidewalk. You know, it's hard to be there and really be there and not begin to absorb that. Of all the places I've been in the world, New Orleans is the only place I've ever been, where if you listen, sidewalks will speak to you."[1] The city is also one of the great international shipping ports and a U.S. center for oil. It's called "the Big Easy" because of the slow motion of the Mississippi River wandering through town.

FINDING THE CITY'S TOTEM SPIRIT

I am speaking about the nature of New Orleans because we needed to access its processmind to help in the midst of chaos. I remembered what I learned in Australia about learning to find the Dreaming of a city (reported in my book *Dreaming While Awake*). Amy and I were doing conflict work between the Aboriginal and more mainstream peoples of Adelaide, Australia. Uncle Lewis (Obrien), an Aboriginal Australian elder, said to Amy and me that the whole city of Adelaide came from the Dreaming—from what I am calling the processmind's hyperspace. He called that Dreaming the "Red Kangaroo." He made a sketch that was published in a city newspaper showing how the entire city of Adelaide, its buildings and roads, was inadvertently organized by the figure of the Red Kangaroo, the spiritual ancestor and totem spirit of the land of Adelaide.[2]

This Aboriginal viewpoint looks at what we have done to the earth, not as good or bad, but as part of the land's Dreaming as organized by its totem spirit. We need contact with that Dreaming—it can help with all of the earth's surface problems. A friend of mine, Dr. Max Schupbach, was told by an "Auntie," an Aboriginal Australian elder woman, "You can kill the kangaroo but not the Kangaroo Dreaming." Similarly, we can "kill" New Orleans but not "New Orleans Dreaming," that is, the earth powers beneath the city.

BROWN POLITICS

I sometimes think of the earth as a deep, subterranean essence of the land that supports all the interactions happening on its surface. The land is a unity that supports the entire diversity of viewpoints—weather conditions, people, animals, plants, waters, and land formations—and their entanglements. As such, the earth has its own power to facilitate the problems that arise between people and the environment.

I want to create a new category of political thought: "brown politics." This concept would embrace the ideology of the green movement, with its focus on ecological and environmental goals, and amplify it with the wisdom of the earth. It would mean working with the problems of individuals, organizations, cities, and nations by reference to the processmind, the totem spirit, the Dreaming, of the land on which they stand.

From this viewpoint, if you must move to a new area, engage first with the processmind, the earth-based totem spirit, of that place. Get to know Grandmother Earth, the Native American reality and deity for our planet. This is also the key to engaging with the people living on that land. People naturally identify with the land on which they live and are often skeptical about people from other areas. I still remember a small village in the Alps I used to visit. Only a few dozen people lived in this village. They rarely engaged with the people in the neighboring village about a half a mile away. When they did, they would say, "The people from that other village are not to be trusted!"

While we all know how dangerously hurtful this xenophobic attitude can be, it also points to something important. From the brown political sense, it encourages people from the "outside" to get to know the land and, through that connection, to relate to the people of that land. I have noticed that if you find your processmind's best spot in a town or village, the people residing there are less likely to perceive you as a "foreigner." If you are connected to a piece of land, at some deep level you are not a foreigner, you are the place.

In any given place, our individual processmind finds the spot that is closest in nature to who we are. Finding this spot that you feel is "yours" is extremely important, because it cues you to behave as if you were at home there. In this way, each of us could live on a particular spot of earth *anywhere* on this earth. Even a jail cell contains an optimal spot, a "power spot," a magical place where you feel the best and feel the closest to your processmind.

Many of us, especially organizational and conflict-resolution facilitators, often work in areas far from home. The suggestion is: Don't work in a new area without knowing how your processmind is linked to the processmind of that place. How do you discover this? Basically, ask where your deepest self is located in your body and then associate that experience with a spot of earth in the new area. If you have yet not been to the place you are going to visit, you have to rely on your imagination of that area and of the specific spot where the deepest part of you might feel the most at home.

For our work in New Orleans, Amy and I did an exercise to experience where our processminds might be located within the city. Here is what happened to Amy. You might want to do a similar exercise for a city or other place where you are going to live, travel, or work. Make notes of your process in #10 on the collage pages, as you have done during the preceding exercises.

EXERCISE 10: THE CITY'S PROCESSMIND

Amy began her process by asking herself, "Where in my body is my deepest self located?" She found it was located in her skull, far behind her eyes. And when she breathed into the experience, it began to rock her back and forth. She then asked where this experience might be located in New Orleans. Having visited New Orleans before, Amy found that the deepest part of herself was located on a particular sidewalk she remembered along the Mississippi River.

In her imagination, Amy went directly to that sidewalk. She stood there and then became that sidewalk area, including the banks of the river and its waters moving slowly through the city. She let the power and presence of that area move her. As she danced, she allowed this sidewalk and riverbank to appear as a human being. To her own surprise, she suddenly imagined not an everyday person but a female "crazy-wisdom" figure, a free-minded person who could follow the changing waves and motions of the river. This figure reminded her of a mystic we had met years earlier standing in another riverfront location, the Mahalakshmi temple in Mumbai, India. Amy's inner crazy-wisdom figure now told her many secrets, such as, "The river flows and everything changes; remain open to all things."

This experience left Amy feeling prepared to help facilitate an open forum on the devastation in New Orleans the next day. I will tell that story shortly. But first, I must mention an amazing event connected to her innerwork. Because of Amy's experience, I investigated the history of that Mahalakshmi temple and found, to my own and Amy's surprise, that it was built after a huge flood in Bombay in 1782 to honor Lakshmi, the Hindu goddess of wealth and prosperity (found also in Jain and Buddhist monuments).

What a marvelous goddess! At that time, Bombay was building levees to protect and connect various parts of what is now called Mumbai. But great storms came, and the levees collapsed several times. According to legend, during one of the storms the engineer who had built those levees had a remarkable dream in which a goddess was lying near the broken levees beneath the water. After the storms, the engineer took a boat to that spot and found a statue of the goddess Lakshmi under the water. He pulled her out, brought her onto the land, and built the temple to honor her. After that, the connecting bridges and levees against the sea could be built; they still exist today.[3]

Having learned this, Amy and I then guessed that her Mississippi processmind totem spirit might be a spirit in New Orleans as well. We were right! After doing some research, we found the water goddess Yemalla in the New Orleans neighborhood on which Amy had meditated! Yemalla is a Yoruba river goddess who cared for the African people brought as slaves from Africa to the United States. She is part of the Yoruba belief system that still exists in New Orleans today among people who practice Yoruba magic and Voodoo.[4] A Voodoo priestess living in New Orleans told us that it was because of the goddess Yemalla that many people were saved from the floods caused by Katrina (see figure 10.2). Yemalla is still helping people "cross the waters" today. Perhaps Amy's Indian-African-American/Lakshmi-Yemalla processmind wisdom figure was trying to come back to our awareness and needs to be honored even today.

Figure 10.2. Rescue in New Orleans after
Hurricane Katrina, 2005.

YEMALLA IN ACTION

Amy's connecting with the water goddess Yemalla and doing her own innerwork helped us with our group-process work in New Orleans. Amy entered into the New Orleans open-forum group process conscious of this water goddess and the spirit of the city. As that group process began, people began discussing, then arguing about, the different sides of the problems and failures. The city had failed. The government, it was said, was racist. People were suffering.

At one point, a person trying to explain the position of those who felt stranded during the hurricane cried out, "I was drowning. I *am* drowning!" An indescribable silence filled in the room. "The government, the people have forgotten me!" she screamed. "Where were you when I was drowning, dying, in need? Could you not hear me, see me, and come and help? Help me! Where were you when we were on the roofs?"

To our surprise, another person stood up and spoke the complacent role. Was this person speaking for himself, or was he acting? We weren't sure. "I am the common citizen. I can't help. I can't come." With our encouragement, he went deeper. "I can't watch any more of this agony, this drowning on TV. I cannot even stand to listen to it on the radio. I can't take more pain. *Leave me alone!* My life is already enough of a mess. Let me be, let me go. Let me close my eyes and my ears! I don't want to help. I can't help."

Again utter stillness pervaded the room. At this point, another New Orleans resident stood up and hesitatingly began moving toward the middle of the forum circle. She did not speak. But Amy, still remembering the figure of Yemalla, intuitively sensed the woman's message and encouraged her to come forward and voice her thoughts. The woman approached the two figures locked in an unresolvable conflict of viewpoints, stood right between them, and voiced her thoughts. Soothingly she said, "Both of you—you who are drowning and you, you who can no longer look—*both* of you are drowning!" She went on addressing both people at the same time, saying, "No one can bear more tragedy. To you both, I say, 'It's *okay*. I am here for both of you.'"

The feeling this woman expressed created a turning point. Both the drowning person and the one who could not face any more pain felt touched, and the one who could not handle the pain began to look at, listen to, and care for the one "drowning." The Yemalla-like compassion of the woman transformed the situation. Everyone felt helped.

That woman embodied a "goddess," and her point was easy to grasp: No one suffers alone. Even the complacent and apparently privileged need help. Without love and being seen, no one can open up to see and feel the needs of others. Openness to the other point of view enabled both sides to work together to take the necessary next steps.

CHAPTER 10

Things to Think About

1. Catastrophic city and world environmental processes may involve pain and death and issues of class and rank, but they also hold the potential for transformation to a new level of understanding and cooperation.
2. To discover your processmind's link to an area, find the deepest part of yourself in your body, imagine how that experience is connected to a real or imagined spot in that area, and let the spirit of that area move you in your work.

CHAPTER 11

THE WORLD IN
YOUR BODY AND YOUR
BODY IN THE WORLD

When we are not in our processmind, we usually experience the world as "out there" and "not me," as sometimes unfamiliar, and often in terms of conflicting parts or even war zones. In this chapter I want to show that we may also experience our body itself as a war zone! When you identify only with your everyday mind, your body may feel like something is attacking you, knocking you out, or injuring your health. On the other hand, body problems can also be nonlocal, that is, belonging to the entire field or situation in which you are living and working. But whether the symptoms are yours or connected nonlocally to the environment, your processmind's nature can facilitate the relief of symptoms as it does outer world conflict situations.

THE ROBOT

We usually identify our body as "local," that is, in the here and now. Irritations or symptoms are usually seen as not right and as things that must be eradicated. This viewpoint regards the body as a mechanical vehicle, a robot. You drive it, and it is supposed to operate perfectly. When it has a problem, repair it. This is a normal and excellent idea. If there is a mechanical or chemical solution to a body problem, and that solution works, all the better. On the other hand, mechanical solutions to body problems do not always work perfectly, perhaps because the body is not only a mechanical device but also a channel for dreamlike experiences, including (but not limited to) your dreams, myths, and processmind. I call the relationship between your physical body and your dream figures the "dreambody" (see my *Dreambody*, *Working with the Dreaming Body*, and *Quantum Mind and Healing*).

In other words, the harmony, conflicts, and battles in which we participate in the outside world and/or in our dreams are not just outside or in our dreams, but are also inside our bodies.

In *Shaman's Body* I point out how shamans in Kenya use their processminds, channeled into shamanic methods, to heal body problems and, at the same time, to heal whole communities. Not just in Africa in the 1980s but throughout time and all over the world, shamans have understood symptoms as an invitation to enter into altered states of consciousness— experiences that were shared with whole communities. Currently, however, the majority of people believe that their body problems are local and have no connection to the community or world. My studies and experiences of shamanism, and the knowledge I've acquired from working with body symptoms over the last forty years, have shown me that body symptoms are inextricably entangled with community processes. Furthermore, just as public situations influence our bodies, working on symptoms may directly or indirectly affect our connection to public life.

In my book *Quantum Mind and Healing*, I introduced the concept of "rainbow medicine" to include medical and bodywork methods, as well as various levels of awareness.[1] The core of process-oriented rainbow medicine is the processmind. Figure 11.1 below, illustrating rainbow medicine, shows how scientific knowledge, rational thinking, sociology, and dreams are all considered possible sources for feeling well or even healing. At the center of the rainbow medicine circle is the "body experience" of the processmind.

Why the name *rainbow medicine*? Most healing and helping procedures are "monochromatic." They stress, as it were, only one color or

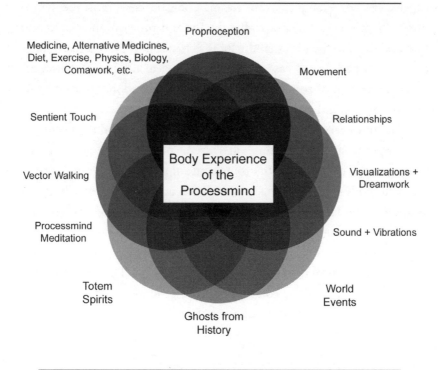

Figure 11.1. Rainbow Medicine.

vibration. The rainbow metaphor encourages us to see any one problem as the center of a rainbow, requiring different viewpoints and levels of awareness and a number of integrated approaches.

Rainbow medicine includes an open interest in both allopathic and teleological procedures. The classical allopathic approach to the body presumes that when something is wrong, it should be fixed. The teleological approach seeks meaning or purpose in what is bugging you. For example, as I said before, from the everyday mind's viewpoint, a symptom may be a chemical or mechanical problem that must be cured. From the processmind's view, this allopathic viewpoint belongs to the present consensus on body symptoms. It can be very important. From another viewpoint, a symptom is a personal and also subjective, dreamlike experience. For example, from the materialistic viewpoint, the symptoms of a cold might be due to the flu. But our processmind might add to this viewpoint the idea that the flu is a chance to explore altered states of consciousness. In any case, from the teleological viewpoint, symptoms may remind you of something you need to know about yourself, your relationships, and the world.

For your everyday mind, following the allopathic and the teleological viewpoints at the same time often seems paradoxical. Either "fix the broken thing" or "listen to the thing's meaning"! But for your processmind, all body events belong to a rainbow, a continuum of vibrations and approaches. If a problem can be fixed mechanically, please do it. And if it contains meaning, let's find it.

The Rainbow medicine figure shows that body experience involves many sensory awareness perceptions or channels. The following list briefly describes the more common sensory grounded channels that are related to our local and nonlocal psychology.

SENSORY GROUNDED CHANNELS

Proprioception. Refers to body sensations, to the feeling of a given symptom. The proprioceptive experience of a symptom (e.g., stabbing pain) is always prefigured in dreams (e.g., a sharp knife—see my book *Dreambody*).

Movement or kinesthesia. Some body experiences express themselves in movement. Movement problems may have a certain rhythm or force that is trying to be expressed.

Relationships. Though "relationship" includes all the other sensory channels, I consider it a channel in its own right because of its significance for body symptoms. Years ago Amy and I worked with a woman who was dying from a brain tumor and had a lot of pain. We thought for sure that she would want to talk about that tumor and the pain. But not at all. She wanted to talk about how she hated her kids! The kids were present, and they did not like her much, either. To our surprise, as we worked with her relationship tension with her kids her pain eased. She felt better.

Visualizations and dreamwork. Visualizing body experience—seeing a feeling, for example—is a form of synaesthesia and is connected to dreams.

Sound, the auditory channel. In some cases, a body experience expresses itself in terms of sound. Auditory proprioceptive synaesthesia can occur, for example, by blowing "healing" sounds into the body, as Aboriginal Australian healers do using the didgeridoo.

Vector walking. All our sensory channels are involved in vector walking, as, for example, when "following the earth." (See *Earth-Based Psychology* for more on this subject.)

Sentient touch. Though sentient touch is a combination of many channels, I include it as a sensory channel unto itself because it is important for people to see, hear, and feel with their hands. Just putting your hand near someone can reveal deep experiences for both you and the other person.

Earlier I said that all the sensory channels overlap. They are "coupled," referring to two or more usually independent processes suddenly influencing each other.[2] For instance, as in the preceding example, relationship situations and body problems are conventionally independent, but they can also be coupled, such that changing a relationship situation can change a body problem, and a particular body experience can change one's ability to relate.

How the world affects your body feeling is also a coupled process. In consensus reality, the world is *not me*. But from the processmind's viewpoint, you are also the world around you. Without the processmind's viewpoint, we might say, "The world bugs me!" or, "You make me sick!" With the processmind's viewpoint, what's happening to us is connected to the environment.

I experienced this interconnection years ago when our Kenyan healers went deep into trance states to heal us. The woman shaman allowed herself to become "possessed" and started to yell, "I am seeing this! I am seeing that!" Then she came up to us and did some magical things. That seemed amazing enough. But then suddenly she began to do the *same* things to the dozen or more people standing around in the circle during our healing ceremony. "Our medicine" was used not just for us but, suddenly, for the whole bush community as well. Her processmind experience (which she attributed to Allah) gave her access to a single world in which we were all entangled and were all helped.

Exercise 11: Public Stress

To understand the how the processmind might connect your body to world events, try the following experiment. Let's focus first on a body experience, on the sense of being stressed by a public situation. Are you ready?

The Stressor. Imagine a public scene where you feel or could have felt stress in your body. If there are several possible scenes, imagine or choose one to begin with. What people or situations seem most stressful to your body during that public event? Imagine, feel, and describe in terms of pictures, feelings, movements, and sounds just what this public "stressor" does to you. Act it out or speak about it, and sketch the stress-making energy.

The Victim. Where in your body do you react to that energy? Is the whole body involved? Where are your symptoms? Feel/sense your body (or possible symptom) reaction and its energy.

Act out this symptom or reaction. What kind of person, or what part of your individual psychology, feels victimized and reacts to the outer stress or "oppressor"? Name and act out this "victim" and sketch its energy.

Your Processmind. Now let's access your processmind. You can do this sitting or standing, but standing is probably best. As you have done in previous exercises in this book, locate your deepest self in your body. Breathe into that area. Then feel it, see it, and let it move you. While in this experience, try to associate it with some real or imaginary earth spot. Go to that spot in your imagination. Look around, and when you are ready, actually become that earth area, that spot, your processmind.

Now shape-shift. Leave your ordinary identity and allow the earth, this processmind spot, to move and dance you. While you are still in the middle of this movement experience, recall the tension-making stressor and the victim's reactions. Still remaining in your processmind experience, look at the stressor and the victim. If you remain in your processmind, it will probably "under-stand" or facilitate the relationship between the stressor and victim processes. This might be a very noncognitive experience. Trust that experience and make a note about how your processmind deals with that polarity in #11 on the collage pages.

While you are still close to your processmind experience, imagine bringing it to another public situation where this same kind of stressor appears. Imagine how your processmind would deal with the stressful situation. Make notes about your experience. In what way could your experience be "medicine," not only for yourself but also for the public situation causing it? Make notes about your insights under #11.

Rachel was a coach who felt stressed by a corporate scene in which she feared men who belittled her. They seemed mean and hard, and she felt oppressed by the way they coldly looked at her. She felt her body react to this public stressor with an anxious fluttering, pounding heart.

Doing this exercise, she found her processmind experience on the Italian Riviera, where, she said, "there were warm sands, amazing tides, and great winds." Just thinking about the warmth and slowness of her Italian coast processmind experience made her feel a lot better.

While she became the Italian Riviera, the men became like the cold sea waves pounding on the sand, making it "shudder." She realized, however, that the beach and the land mass behind it were so huge that the cold sea did not have much effect on the warm seashore. She saw that her processmind included both the shuddering embankment and the pounding of the waves in one process. "Wow, it's all me, it's all simply nature! I too can be cold and almost threatening sometimes! And then I am also warm-hearted." These thoughts made her laugh and relieved her anxiety and heart symptoms.

Rachel had no trouble imagining how to use this Italian Riviera processmind experience at the corporation's next event. The next time she met those men, she, like the beach, would simply shudder and flow with the cold waves coming in and then be cool and powerful herself. A few weeks later, she actualized this experience and used this "medicine." She reported: "I found myself at first shuddering again in the presence of those men. Then I remembered that I am both the warm land and cold sea. So I rolled back and forth, and was also cooler and much more forceful than usual. To my surprise, I felt warmer toward myself and toward everyone else as well! The others seemed to respect me more."

Outer situations create tensions and illnesses in part because we don't see the outer situations and our resistance to them as parts of the diversity of our own processmind. Once Rachel saw that both the stressor and victim—both the feared coldness and the anxiety—were contained as phases and parts of her processmind "Riviera" field, her body was able to help her business work.

Figure 11.2. The Italian Riviera as a Totem Earth Spot.

MYTHOSTASIS

If you were able to have a processmind experience by doing this exercise, it may have given you at least a flickering sense of wellness. The processmind's wellness is more than the simple well-being of the body and the mind. Let me explain. Physical well-being is characterized by homeostasis, which is the property of either an open or closed system, especially a living organism, that regulates its own internal environment so as to maintain a stable, constant condition.[3] For example, if you get hot, your body sweats to cool off and maintain a more or less steady temperature. Allostasis is biological homeostasis but also includes the behavioral and psychological means to create homeostasis. For example, if someone is chasing you, to protect yourself you automatically sweat, and you also run to remain safe. Allostatic change encompasses all the possible adaptations we go through to adjust and live through social, ecological, and world stress in order to achieve homeostasis.[4]

Homeostasis and allostasis are the processmind's physiological and psychological processes that protect life. However, the processmind's goal includes but goes beyond these. The processmind maintains our *mythic* nature. I define *mythostasis* as the processmind's ability to create social, behavioral, and biological-change processes to maintain and stabilize our biology *and* maintain contact with our basic nature. Mythostasis is our ability to deal with stress by being variable, zigzagging between polarities, following positive and negative feedback from the environment while remaining mythic selves—close to our basic big U direction and processmind. Rachel's experiences from the preceding exercise and Sara Halprin's last experiences before dying, described in chapter 1, suggest that the processmind is mythostatic both during life and at the edge of life, when allostasis and homeostasis fail.

The processmind's mythostasis sustains homeostasis and self-organizes body processes that maintain our basic myth even when life itself seems endangered or near death. Likewise, the mythostasis of a group, an organization, or a city keeps it close to its earth-based nature. Mythostasis appears in the Aboriginal Australian idea mentioned in chapter 10: "You can kill the kangaroo, but not the kangaroo Dreaming." Mythostasis includes physiology but may well go beyond physical life functions to maintain our essence. In Rachel's case, her processmind's mythostasis used the Italian beach and her basic Italian Riviera direction in life to achieve homeostasis.

The processmind's mythostatic flow brings back the sense of overall wellness. Near death, when the allostasis needed to reach homeostasis begins to fail, the overarching paradigm of mythostasis becomes more apparent, maintaining our connection to a mythic, totem spirit core. It has often seemed to me that many symptoms and perhaps aging itself promote awareness of the processmind's mythostatic power. As we come to grips with the fact that our consensus-reality identity is unsustainable, limited (at present) to 120 years maximum, something in us reminds us that life in some form continues. You can kill the kangaroo but not its Dreaming.

Recall Feynman's diagram as represented in chapter 9 (figure 9.1), which allowed us to imagine how the processmind flows both forward

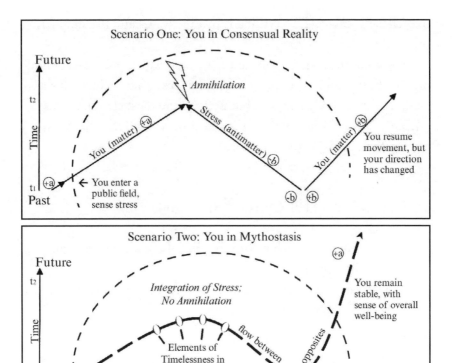

Figure 11.3. Mythostasis, as adapted from Richard Feynman's diagrams. In consensus reality, you may meet opposition (stress), but in the processmind's mythostatic space you flow between opposites and so remain stable.

and backward in time. Applying that diagram to stressful situations, we can recognize the dashed, timeless processmind line as mythostasis. From the consensus-reality viewpoint, going forward in time your body stress is due to oppressive symptom-creators—that is, to stress factors that threaten to "annihilate" you. But if your everyday identity relaxes enough to find your processmind, the dashed, timeless processmind process in Feynman's diagram appears. It allows your awareness to facilitate and flow between one side or energy and its opposition. To use Rachel's language, everything is just the waves and the shuddering beach of the Riviera.

We are individuals in time and space, and we are also one continuous, mythostatic time-free process.[5] Our processmind facilitates the alleviation of inner body tensions, but perhaps the most complete sense of "wellness" occurs when we also use our processmind to help the world resolve its tensions as well.

Things to Think About

1. Your body is a machine or robot but also a dream and a piece of the whole world.
2. Life can be stressful, but our mythostatic processmind nature swings with just about anything.

THE PROCESSMIND IN SCIENCE AND RELIGION

The most beautiful thing we can experience is the mysterious. It is the source of all true art and all science. He to whom this emotion is a stranger, who can no longer pause to wonder and stand rapt in awe, is as good as dead: his eyes are closed.

— Albert Einstein

CHAPTER 12

SCIENCE, RELIGION, AND GOD EXPERIENCE

In the first two parts of this book, we explored the qualities of the processmind and how to remain in the semi-altered state of consciousness I call "half in, half out" while sensing and applying this new (or ancient) form of consciousness to moods, symptoms, relationships, conflict, and public situations. Now, in part three, we will consider how immersing yourself in the processmind's unitive consciousness might influence your view of science, religion, and their interconnection. In this chapter I want to explore belief systems in general and the nature of your belief system in particular: how it gives meaning to your life and how it needs your awareness to really "work."

THE EDGE BETWEEN SCIENCE AND RELIGION

Science and religion are divided, but not as much so as some may think. In a general way, science is like religion insofar as scientists believe in a highest principle: the existence of patterns appearing in the measurements of space, time, and matter. Besides a highest principle, science also has a ritual: using the scientific method to test theories in measurable, laboratory settings. Extraneous theories that do not help to understand a given event are sidelined. In a way, science is the religion of consensus reality, which believes that space, time, and material events are organized by patterns that some call the "mind of God."

Because science marginalizes subjective experiences—that is, non-measurable effects—it is not satisfying to everyone. Many people need myth and meaning, or at least some kind of feeling, to make their lives worthwhile. I call the world of myth and meaning, of dreams and transcendent subjective experience, "dreamland" or "the essence." A process-oriented approach to events includes both science and spirituality, that is, measurable reality as well as dream and essence-dimension experiences. Any situation combines all levels. For example, the piece of earth constituting a garden is a real thing. There is a science to gardening. You need to know what to plant and when. At the same time, some gardeners maintain a certain feeling about that piece of earth that transforms the science of gardening into an art. That feeling can't quite be measured or even defined. For the gardener, the time, space, matter, and dreams about the garden are inseparable. In a way, science and spiritual traditions are connected for the gardener as different dimensions of the same thing.

Since its discovery in the 1970s, empirical evidence of nonlocality in quantum theory has brought physics and religion closer to one another. Classical Newtonian physics, which defines locality in terms of separate spaces and times, borders on quantum physics, which studies nonlocality—that is, interconnected parts that cannot be considered independently of one another no matter how separated they are in time or space. Nonlocality is close to an essence ingredient in most religions: the sense that something like an intelligent, unified field connects everyone and everything. Moreover, physics and religions both have their theories—the word *theory* being connected to *speculation*, to *theion* (meaning "divine things"), and to contemplating the divine organization (or "cosmos") of nature. Both physics and religions have stories, dreams, and truths about nature. Both seek to answer questions such as "Who am I?" "Why am I here?" and "Who is asking these questions?" Both seek to know the intelligent agent behind the universe, which scientists other than Einstein have associated with the Divine. The well-known astrophysicist Stephen Hawking said recently, for example: "If we do discover a theory of everything . . . it would be the ultimate triumph of human reason—for then we would truly know the mind of God."[1]

THE UNIVERSE AS AWARENESS LEVELS

From one standpoint, we can conjecture: Perhaps one aspect of the mind of God is divined by "human reason," as Hawking calls the scientific method, while another aspect of that same mind of God is known through contemplation, innerwork, and awareness during altered states of consciousness. The consensus-reality universe in physics includes everything that can be measured and recorded, that is, everything that physically exists: the entirety of space and time and all forms of matter, energy, and momentum, as well as the laws and their associated constants. In consensus reality, measurements tell us that the universe began about 13.7 billion years ago. Yet, the consensus reality view does not tell us how the universe began, or even if the word *beginning* is anything more than a time-based cultural concept of today. Concepts like "beginning" and "ending" are not always applicable in a quantum world, where time can reverse.

The edge between consensus reality and dreamland, between science and religion, is like an edge between two worlds. The famous Flammarion woodcut (from Camille Flammarion's *L'atmosphère: Météorologie Populaire*, a book on meteorology meant for the general French public of 1888) illustrates this beautifully (see figure 12.1). The visible, known world is the inner sphere on the right-hand side of the picture, while another realm, perhaps a dreaming or spiritual universe, is to the left and beyond. A man peers through the earth's atmosphere as if it were a curtain to look at the workings of the universe. The picture's original caption, translated into English, says: "A medieval missionary tells that he has found the point where heaven and Earth meet."

Figure 12.1. *L'atmosphère:*
Météorologie Populaire. Woodcut by
Camille Flammarion, 1888.

This woodcut shows the observer in the condition I call "half in, half out"—half in "heaven" and half on "earth." Seen psychologically, the conflict between science and religion can be mapped exactly on this edge between awareness of consensus reality facts and details, and connection to dreamland and processmind. Neither science nor religion can bridge this gap on its own; in fact, because one is committed to consensus-reality "Earth" and the other to the reality of "heaven," the gap only enhances the difference between these two viewpoints. This separation makes us suffer.

The processmind is able to straddle the edge between science and religion because it allows for and encompasses multidimensional experience. This is the value of connecting to the processmind. It is the one who can "paint" that "woodcut." For the processmind, the universe is both a measurable concept and a subjective experience.

As we saw earlier, the universe appears in the math of quantum physics and also in the "flirts" of psychology as a self-reflecting intelligence trying to look at itself. I use the term *universe* to mean the sum of all consensus reality and dreamlike mythic experiences—a self-organizing, self-reflective intelligence. This definition includes the field theories of physics and religious stories and myths about the cosmos as well as ineffable mystical "oneness" experiences. The universe seems to be an objective thing from the consensus-reality perspective, but it is also a process that is constantly wondering about itself, articulating and rediscovering itself through people. This self-discovery process inextricably and inexorably connects physics and psychology. To say this more simply: *the universe is the sum of all the changing viewpoints about it.*

Why am I focusing on what the universe is or is not? Most people don't think about this topic unless they have spiritual experiences or are mystics, crazy scientists, or near death. My primary reason is to reduce the suffering we feel when we identify ourselves as only one part of nature, one part of the universe. To be only a part is to be in constant conflict with other parts. Stay half in and half out of the altered state of the processmind to appreciate and facilitate the other parts in consensus reality.

Processmind's First and Second Training in Science and Religion

Who can deal with the entire universe? Well, no one can or should have to do so. On the other hand, everyone does and must, simply because we live in the universe—it is our home! Any such training must be deeply democratic, that is, the training must value both facts and figures, as well as the dreaming and sentient essence levels of things. We need first, a disciplined training to notice facts, figures, signals, roles, flirts, and feedback.[2] Then we need a second training on how to sense and follow experiences that cannot always be verbalized.

In the first training, watch signals and check things out; notice what is happening at the visible and auditory levels. If you don't understand, ask. Use your rational, cognitive mind as much as possible. Be mechanical and "realistic." Base your behavior in part on known facts, medicines, good ideas, tested concepts. However, doubt everything you hear until you have tested and validated it with your own experience.

In the second training, learn about your processmind through some form of meditation that opens your mind to subtle experience. Or use some of the training exercises in this book. Since our awareness naturally goes back and forth between reality and dreaming, being half in and half out can be learned, but not always easily described in words. The second training is paradoxical. It happens. Producing processmind experiences both is and is not "learnable"—at least, in the cognitive sense. Some people seem to grow into knowing and using the deepest part of themselves in everyday life. However, just about everyone I have worked with near death, whether they were spiritual believers or ardent rationalists, experienced some form of transcendence. In other words, whether they knew about the processmind or not, the processmind emerged and made sense out of even seemingly chaotic events.

Although there is a first-level training aspect to learning about the processmind, you can't force yourself to be in the processmind experience all the time. Nor, do I feel, is it a "moral duty" in any sense. However, sensing your processmind as always present can be helpful, for it is in fact present behind all states of consciousness, both the most rational, doubtful, disrespectful mind and the "spiritual" type of mind.

PROCESSMIND AS THE WHOLE STORY

The processmind is present during good as well as dreadful times. I learned this for the first time on the way to kindergarten and first grade. I was born in 1940 in the United States, and my earliest years were filled with radio reports about war in some distant place. Perhaps because my parents were Jewish they were afraid to speak about religion, or perhaps it was because they wanted me to grow up in a secular world. I never heard about religion during the first six years of my life. My first shocking understanding of the word *God* was the thought: "God must be a gang leader." Why did I think that? Because a gang of children and young adults who wanted to kill me on the way to school claimed that my people had killed their "God" and they were seeking revenge by "destroying" me. I told them I thought they had the wrong person; I did not know any such people as "my people." But they thought otherwise.

It took me quite a while, but today I can say those "hurtful" people were some of my greatest teachers, even while they were dreadful. I experienced how close God could bring me to death but also to life. The African Americans watching from a safe distance what was happening to me inside of that gang of fighters were afraid to get involved because they were so outnumbered. Still, these brave people cheered me on, saying, "Don't give up, don't lie there on the ground and get kicked. They'll kill you! You must stand up again and fight!" Their supportive voices seemed to be transmitting love from another dimension. That situation taught me an unforgettable lesson.

Today I realize that fear and hate are natural but they are not the whole story. I realize that what most people call "God" is only part of a story, the so-called good part, yet there is something greater than that good part. There is something that puts all the parts together. What I now call "God" is the whole story, not a part of it.

To respect those who may be hurt if I say that God is all dimensions, both good and evil, I won't use the "G" term that way again. Instead, I'll say that the *processmind* is neither good nor evil but the whole story, which includes all the parts. It was the processmind that hurt me even while it was saying, "Come on, get up and live." The divine intelligence in our universe shows itself not only as one state or energy, not only as one figure, but as all the states and all the figures needed to create the story. Processmind is the whole story, including the suffering that drives us to know of its existence. Once you know of the intelligence behind difficult situations, like body symptoms and outer conflicts, life is easier, at least for a moment. The more we know about the processmind, the more we can enable the worst stories to evolve into more enriching ones.

EXERCISE 12A: PROCESSMIND AS THE WHOLE STORY

I warmly recommend that you think about something dreadful that happened to you. Who or what was involved? What occurred? How long ago was it? If you are able to explore the whole story, then recall the events. Imagine what it was that allowed and helped you to survive those worst experiences. Ask yourself or your dreaming mind just how you managed to survive. If you don't know, let yourself create a spontaneous dreamlike solution.

Even if your life was shortened by some terrible experience, how have you survived until now? What great force was behind that "trouble"? Give it a name. Let that spirit explain its name, if it can. Remember the earlier processmind experiences in this book, or look at your collage page in appendix B to recall some of your processmind insights. Could your processmind somehow have been behind what happened? Please make a note about this for yourself under #12a on the collage page.

These questions remind me of the story of Naropa that I told in chapter 8. His teacher, Tilopa, told Naropa at the last moment that all the problems of his life, even the near-death experiences, were Tilopa himself, helping Naropa learn to detach.

Each of us has her or his own process wisdom that can communicate its reasons and intents. The pragmatic effect of seeing the processmind as the whole story, as the ongoing process, is that we are more likely to accept and also go beyond vengeance or depression about life's troubles. From our everyday perspective, things are either bad or good. From the processmind's perspective, nothing is absolutely bad or good. Everything is happening within the context of an overall story direction, a powerful story

Figure 12.2. Processmind as a Story Line.

trying to create greater awareness. Figure 12.2 shows how the overall story line direction encompasses all the zigzags, including difficult life events.

RELIGIOUS DIRECTIONS

As individuals, we each have a story line, a big U, with many diverse directions. We are the overall story, as well as all its parts. Our scientific and religious organizations and belief systems are the same. They too have a story line, a big U. That U is the group's mythic direction, corresponding to the group's essence. That direction, or the processmind power creating that direction, is one of the main reasons we follow or believe in that organization or tradition and its stories, rules, and ethics.

As I said earlier, I originally developed the big U idea in response to the quantum wave function and Richard Feynman's quantum electrodynamics. In my book *Earth-Based Psychology*, I spoke about how David Bohm saw that wave function as a pilot wave guiding a ship on the water. The quantum wave function's vector-psychological counterpart is the big U, the ship's most likely overall, or mythostatic, direction. For example, it allows a ship to vacillate at times and go to the right, the left, or even backward. My point is that all organizations, including religions, have a big U that represents the overall direction or essence of the organization. In principle, an organization's or religion's deepest beliefs are a kind of pilot wave moving it through all of its stories.

Most members of organizations (i.e., most "believers") often forget or don't follow the original spiritual or mystical essence of the organization but instead reside in consensus reality, where they depend upon rules and "commandments" to lead their lives. People who don't follow these rules, either because they don't agree or because they belong to other groups, are usually considered "bad people." They are the "troublemakers," "doubters," or "nonbelievers," who are going in the "wrong" direction. They must be turned back on the right path!

You can see in figure 12.3 that the "good" and "bad" directions are zigzags—that is, part of the overall story direction, U. From this larger perspective all parts are needed, and there is no absolute good or bad. The U includes, even needs, the diversity of zigzag possibilities to add up to its overall direction. All parts are needed to co-create the meaning of an organization, of religious institutions. All parts together sum up to the idea of "God," or whatever the highest principle is called.

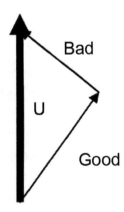

Figure 12.3. The Good, the Bad, and the U in Religion.

Think of the Garden of Eden story. From the processmind viewpoint, God, Adam, Eve, the serpent, and tree are mythic figures, dreamland figures and concepts constituting not only parts but different phases of the same story. The ground of Eden "supports" all of these voices. Seen as a process, the Garden of Eden story tells us that it is natural to create a new world, then to make rules, then to doubt the rules and the creator, and finally to create new levels (and fall to Earth).

I realize that this is not a very common view of things. It takes a processmind perspective to see conflicts as helping to define the wealth— that is, the diversity—of an institution or group.

MONOLATRISM

Let's apply the processmind perspective to biblical commandments. A central rule characteristic of monotheisms is that believers should not be interested in other gods. But the god telling us this is also telling us that there *are* other gods. This implies that god as a concept is but one part of a conflict story. The other gods are "bad." In essence, the "good" god is telling "his" people that they must *not* follow other "directions."

From a processmind viewpoint, commandments are dreamland or consensus-reality prescriptions "handed down" by the processmind world; they are not the essence themselves. Moses went up the mountain and got commandments from an otherwise ineffable source. These commandments are the origin of an ethics "handed down," and at the same time, the origin of inner conflicts and religious wars. "Have no other gods before me!" The directions represented by the god speaking and the "other gods" include all the tensions that are needed to express the diversity and mystery behind the universe—that is, the mind of God.

A monolatrist is someone who worships one god but believes that other versions of god exist. Such an individual probably knows or intuits that the processmind is the essence of all dreamland god concepts. A monotheist can be a monolatrist as long as she or he finds the mystical essence of her or his beliefs and realizes that the images of the highest principles depend upon the communities, cultures, and times involved. A monolatrist can say, "I believe in my God, and I also understand yours and the beliefs and stories about yours." From a processmind viewpoint, a monolatrist would even say, "My God is also an aspect of mine!"

Monolatrists as well as polylatrists (worshippers of several religions) are in fact a large part of the population.[3] Furthermore, we all go through different moods and phases wherein we may be atheistic, monotheistic, monolatrist, and so on, at different moments.

MOTHER TERESA'S MISSING GOD

The processmind idea might have been helpful to Mother Teresa, the remarkable Roman Catholic nun who won the Nobel Peace Prize for her work with the poor, sick, orphaned, and dying. Apparently, she sometimes complained bitterly that when she needed God, "he" was not always there. Just before beginning her work in the slums of Calcutta, she wrote: "Where is my faith? Even deep down there is nothing but emptiness and darkness. If there be a God—please forgive me."[4]

Years later she still expressed a "deep longing for God" and said she felt "repulsed, empty, no faith, no love, no zeal." And then: "What do I labor for? If there be no God, there can be no soul. If there be no soul then, Jesus, You also are not true."

To me, her doubts belong to the diversity of her processmind communicating through her everyday mind about itself to another part of itself. It was saying: I am also emptiness and darkness, and I, too, lose track of myself. I, too, have forgotten and just "labor," for I know not what reason. Jesus himself, the one to whom she is devoted, also doubted God for a moment in his famous lament on the cross, "My God, my God, why have you forsaken me?" For me Mother Teresa's words are pointing to another aspect of the whole Christ story, the aspect about doubt.

Mother Teresa reminds me of the process of one of my students. But before I tell her story, I invite you to try the following exercise to explore the process involved in your own belief systems.

EXERCISE 12B: YOUR BELIEF PROCESSES

Begin by recalling your greatest beliefs or highest principles. Note one of them in #12b on the collage page. To which, if any, organization or organizations are your beliefs connected? If there are several organizations, which might be closest to your own belief system? What is one of the most problematic aspects of that organization?

Let's see now what, if anything, your dreaming adds to your belief system. Think of your belief again. Close your eyes for a moment. Then let them slowly open. Gaze slowly around you. Notice what catches your attention. If there are several things, let your unconscious mind tell you on which to focus. Study this "flirt" to know what it "says" to you. What does this add, if anything, to your belief system? Take note.

Now meditate on and feel the earth underneath and around you, and let the earth show you the central direction, the big U of your beliefs. Walk in that direction (or use your pencil to "walk" on paper) to experience the meaning/feeling of that direction. How might this walking experience appear as a dream image or images plus waking feelings? How has this direction been a guide and creator in your personal life? Follow and feel this direction in your body and movement to understand its message.

Now consider: What do you follow when you don't follow your big U belief vector, that is, your highest principles? Ask the earth to show you the vector direction of your nature when you don't follow your highest principles. Is it connected in any way with the "problematic aspects" of the organization you noted earlier in this exercise? Walk your big U belief vector again, and while walking that line, notice how it deals with the direction that does not follow your highest principles. Make notes in #12b.

THE FOREST'S LESSON

One of my students related the experiences she had with this exercise. She had been suffering because she was pushing to do things all the time and could not find and follow her deepest direction, which was her belief in the "deep green forests" of the northwestern United States. During the exercise, her belief's big U vector appeared as the direction toward that part of the country, which she associated with the trees in Oregon's forests. "They are amazing; they survive the storms and twist, sway, and grow more beautiful and amazing with each storm," she said. Then looking sad, she complained about the part of her that did not believe and "would not follow this direction." This part, she said, "just pushes blindly ahead!"

As she walked again along the big U direction of her beloved forests, she meditated on that direction and asked herself, "How would this direction deal with the pusher in me?" The direction answered, "No problem; push more! Forget all that you believe in and just push until you are exhausted! That is how trees grow. Forests need the storms of life to create both fallen trees and new growth!"

She realized that pushing was just one of the forest's storms, and she cried, saying that until now, she had been against the "pushiness" part of herself and hated pushy people in institutions! "Those kinds of people were just bad!"

This work brought out the monolatrist in her—a believer in mainly one principle (the forest) who also recognized and accepted other aspects of that principle (the pusher, the storms). As a monolatrist, she understood for a moment that her highest principle, her "God," appeared in both "good" and "bad" weather.

THINGS TO THINK ABOUT

1. Science and religion are not as split as they appear.
2. From the processmind viewpoint, science and religion are different dimensions of a worldview that includes both everyday reality and dreaming.
3. From the processmind viewpoint, God is the whole story, not just one of its parts.
4. God emerges into consensus reality as a concept, a belief, and a lawmaker who has opponents.
5. What we call trouble may be the processmind showing its diversity.

YOUR (EARTH-BASED) ETHICS

We have been considering how the processmind manifests as a story of events, including the "good" and the "bad" parts. We can also think of the processmind as manifesting the entire story of creation. In this sense, God (as the universe's processmind) is the origin of the universe and also the interaction between the universe's parts. Physics, too, has stories about the creation of the universe and has come up with terms for the universe's beginning, such as "Big Bang," "ground state" or "zero-point field," the "mind of God," and the "observer effect."[1]

But who cares about how the universe got created? Most of us have enough body problems, financial woes, and relationship trouble to think about! If the creation of the universe is not foremost on your mind, my suggestion is to not worry about it and just do whatever works best for you. However, if your life is not satisfying or meaningful to you, it may be time to ponder the larger patterns behind life in order to develop goals and ethics that align with those patterns. Ethics in the general sense is related to your view of what it means to lead a satisfying life. From a processmind standpoint, your ethics are linked to your sense of why you are on this earth and how close you are living to your deepest self. Ethics is not just a philosophical topic but a processmind experience.

Think about both the negative and the positive attitudes you bring to working with yourself, with others in relationships, with business problems. Do those attitudes work? How do you deal with friends who cause you conflict or betray you, or with groups that contradict the groups to which you belong? Do you assume that there is an absolute "good" or "bad"? Your beliefs and ethics guide your behavior in all the things that you do, usually unconsciously. If you follow your ethics consciously, you are more likely to feel that your life is worthwhile, or at least that you are contributing to a meaningful universe and a rich and interactive world.

Most scientists would agree that science tells us how to make bombs but not whether we should go to war. Even if "sticking to the facts" is part of your ethics, facts alone are rarely sufficient to lead a meaningful life. Most spiritual traditions suggest that we should help others and conduct ourselves in a "good" manner that does not cause harm. While these ethical guidelines, intended to be clear about what to do and not do, are enough for many, they are often at odds with what we know about the dream world and physical universe. A quick glance at the environmental, national, and international conflicts around us suggests that we need some new directions in getting along with one another and the natural world. To participate in creating a world we feel good about, each needs to be in touch with his and her own sense of what is behind creation.

ENTANGLED CO-CREATION

One thing I know for sure from my own and other people's deep experiences, in both my private practice and international conflict work, is that *who or what you experience, experiences you.* The observer and the observed experience each other and thereby co-create reality. According to the transactional approach to quantum physics, reality occurs through the medium of quantum waves or dreamlike flirts.[2] Reality comes about through a process of reflection! Every time we look at something, we participate in creating the universe and, in a way, it expands from nothing to something. The late and great physicist John Wheeler called this the "participatory universe." The past, the future, and the present, containing you and me, are here in part, according to Wheeler, because the universe is participatory. We co-create it together.[3] In other words, the universe brings itself into being through becoming observers that reflect, thereby helping to create reality.

I call this connection between the observer and the observed "entangled co-creation." We experience this in relationships. Have you not noticed how the other person's face changes in response to how yours changes? We experience it in dreams, too. What you dream has somehow already experienced you, and it changes accordingly, as you can tell by the next night's dreams. So also with religion: As the human race grows older, its images of the divine change as well (see figure 13.1). These images influence us, we change . . . and so it goes.

This creation-feedback-recreation process can be seen in our zigzagging from one direction to another throughout personal life and history. The zigzag paths themselves are entangled and co-creative, yet their overall path seems to be organized by a big U vector, the processmind. The names given for the processmind vary depending upon the culture and times. I have mentioned at various points in this book, for example, Unkulunkulu, Buddha nature, God, Jesus, Allah, Zen mind, totem spirits, and others. Regardless of these and other names, the processmind is the

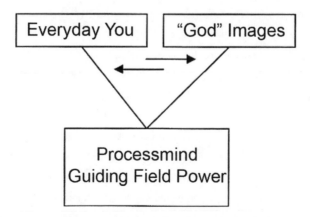

Figure 13.1. Entangled Co-creation.

force field behind both the story and storyteller. We experience ourselves normally only as the storyteller, not realizing how the story influences us. Moreover, we sense even less the processmind power that gave rise to both the storyteller and the story, the observer and observed, the worshipper and the image of the divine. The images and stories change over time, the facts and formulation of the highest principles change as communities evolve, but the organizing power and direction of the earth's field behind them changes less or not at all.

Entangled co-creation appears in dreamwork as well. To understand one of your dreams, it is rarely enough to understand even the clearest dream image. To truly comprehend a dream, you need to know exactly for whom that image is meant, and you need to know what you were feeling before going to bed. Dreams arise in part as a response to what you were thinking and feeling. In other words, dreams do what they do in part because of what you did. That's entanglement! Entangled co-creation implies that the *entire relationship process is the point*. Neither "you" nor "it" is the point. It's all about you, it, and the processmind field between us; that is our *entangled co-creation*.

The generalization from dreamwork is that the face of the divine is changed by those who create or dream it.[4] Thus, the deepest principle, Suzuki's dark field in chapter 1, may not appear in any one of the stories, parts, or images but appears as the power behind the interactions and changes in both observer and observed.

The same may be true for our physical world as well. You, as an observer, change the world just by touching it. Think about macrophysics. Think about your body. As a patient, you see your doctor or nurse for your annual checkup. The nurse uses a thermometer and touches your ear to take your temperature. What do you think happens to the temperature of the thermometer? If the thermometer was at room temperature of, let's say, 72 degrees Fahrenheit, the thermometer has to warm up to show the temperature of your body. To do that, the thermometer heats up using energy from your body and, in doing so, cools down your ear and your body. The amount of heat you lose is so little that no one thinks about it. However, in principle, every measurement you make, everything you touch, every breath you breathe changes the world. That's the observer effect. The thermometer does not measure your temperature, but the temperature, you, and the thermometer (and medical helpers) "co-create." Even your desire to observe or touch somebody or something changes the world.

The observer effect occurs at quantum levels as well. To see a sub-atomic particle you need little tiny photons of light. That is, seeing a particle requires another particle. This means that when you look at a particle, you don't just disturb it a little; other particles need to bombard it. This disturbance lies behind the uncertainty principle: what you see is changed by your looking at it. In short, we don't know anything for sure about anything! We cannot get a "true," unchanging piece of information, such as the location at a particular time of a particular particle. What we are viewing instead is our ongoing, entangled co-creative process with that particle. There are no fixed "things"; there is only entangled co-creation, whose subtle background is the processmind.

The Ethics of Entangled Co-creation

The existence and experience of co-creativity give rise to an ethics that embraces the idea of a separate you and me and is also aware of the ongoing entanglement process and the capacity of the processmind to choreograph and flow with all its parts. This translates into preparing to do something, and then forgetting the preparation and following your processmind as it swings from one aspect or energy to another.

Ethics are to morals approximately as theory is to practice. Your morals—how you put your ethics into practice—depend entirely upon the processes of the moment and the nature of your processmind. When I ask myself what it means to have a fulfilling personal life, or what will help an individual, community, or organization, I think of "following my/their processes." That is my ethics: find my own and help others find and follow their own entangled co-creative processes. I am happiest that way, and others in my life are most likely to succeed as well. This perspective seems to work for all facilitators who work with individuals, organizations, and large group conflicts. Find the processmind of the situation and use it to swing with the various roles, sides, individuals, and issues as the process of co-creation occurs.

Community processes often revolve around identifying and trying to change "bad" people. Let's think about this from a processmind viewpoint. Imagine a community whose members believe in "working together" but one of their members is totally self-centered. Often the response is: "She (or he) is not following the rules and must be warned or fined in some way!" However, if they shifted to a process-oriented ethics, the group members could instead use their community processmind awareness to see that "wanting to be self-centered and doing things *my* way" could be an important role. Perhaps the "bad" person is bringing this viewpoint forward for everyone to consider. Likewise, perhaps the individual is dreaming up the community in order to have to engage with rules. Both the community and the individual are in the midst of a entangled co-creation that goes beyond "good" or "bad" to the point where everyone is enriched by the definitive nature of doing things *my* way.

THE DEATH WALK

Now consider an individual following his or her deepest ethics who wants to do something new but is part of a rigid community. What happens to that individual? The rigid community, unable to swing with the situation and afraid of being destroyed by such an individual, usually fights back. The individual can see this as a potential disaster but also as an opportunity to change the world. How?

In his book *Journey to Ixtlan*, Carlos Castaneda tells a wonderful story about this very issue that I retold in my book *Shaman's Body*. I called the process of such a warrior the "death walk."[5] According to Castaneda's shaman teacher, don Juan Matus, once upon a time there were warriors who decided they did not agree with the rules of their warrior organization. Being themselves, the warriors had to disobey those rules. But being itself, the organization also had to punish them. The organization confronted the rebels and told them they had one last chance. The rule breakers had to walk in front of the "jury," who had their guns aimed to kill.

As the jurors drew their guns to shoot, the warriors walked in front of them in such a manner that they could not pull their triggers. What happened? Don Juan and Castaneda never tell us the details. But perhaps the warriors were so much in contact with their own earth-based ethics that they could feel how their processmind included not only their own behavior but also the organization's.

I can imagine, for example, that they understood how the group's behavior was something they needed, and also how their behavior could profit them and the group. They accomplished this not by trying to convince the group but by following their innermost selves beyond any concept such as "power," leadership, strength, or even truth. The warriors were one with the overall process, including their own obstreperousness. In my mind, they not only survived but consciously enabled entangled co-creation to appear. They were right and wrong, the others were wrong and right, and, in a way, "right and wrong" became irrelevant as a deeper, more unitive entangled co-creative experience emerged. The warrior—any individual with enough awareness to find her or his deepest processmind ethics—represents not only herself or himself, but the earth as well. Such people together with the organization and the earth create a more conscious future through entangled co-creation.

Exercise 13: Finding Your Own Ethics

Everyone can find benefit in determining their deepest ethics. Take notes in what follows and include them in #13 on the collage page. Relax for a moment, and then we can start.

To begin, note one or two moral or ethical problems that are on your mind these days—however you define *morals* and *ethics*. Then make a note about the ethics you try to follow in your everyday life. What are they? Do you try to be "good," care for others, care for family members, be a loyal group member? After noting your everyday ethics, ask yourself about your hidden ethics— those unwritten rules you follow without admitting them to yourself or others. For example, do you seek power? Are you greedy? And so on. Don't skip the "bad" ones; just accept their presence. Make notes about your answers and then let's go on.

Now, remember or sense your deepest self somewhere in your body and breathe into that area. What earth spot might be associated with this experience? Be that earth spot and take your time meditating as that spot. Let it move you and or prompt you to make sounds. What kind of "knowing" do you sense from the spot and the area around it? Continue meditating on your processmind experiences until they teach you something you can use in everyday life. Please make note of this processmind teaching.

What belief system and ethics, if any, arise from this processmind, earth-based ethics experience? Did your experience include in some way your "hidden" ethics as well as the more familiar everyday ones? Finally, how might what you discovered during this experience help you deal with the moral and ethical problems you identified at the beginning? What action, if any, is suggested? Again, make notes under #13 on your collage page.

BEYOND FIGHTING, LOSING, AND WINNING

A student of mine, let's call him John, meditated on exercise 13 and then shared what he had learned. He had a problem with a powerful and sometimes brutal family member. John did not want to get angry and shout at him, and thus behave just like him, but he could not stand the person. During the exercise John saw that his own "unwritten ethics" were to shout and get angry, just like those of his family member.

He also found that his deepest ethics were to follow what he called "Jesus, my heart." To the surprise of his everyday mind, this ethics included his unwritten ethics. To follow "Jesus, my heart," John had to sometimes be loud and angry like the family member he disliked! He saw that Jesus was open to the "tough" part of himself and to the same expression from the family member. His heart understood, but it seemed paradoxical to his everyday mind. How could he be strong without that being an end unto itself? Then his Jesus heart explained it. Being strong would help him and everyone else realize that strength is not what counts. Strength was fine, but it was not the point. Love would always be present, even in anger.

Shortly thereafter, he met that aggressive family member. John cried as he told me later what happened:

> I decided to be tough and fight, remembering that love, not strength, was the major point. I yelled back at him but he was much stronger. As I was losing, something strange happened. I heard myself telling my opponent that he was so strong that nothing but God could save me now. Of all the crazy things, he started to cry! We both cried and then hugged each other.

John said that after that experience, he was no longer afraid of this man. Being open to power while remembering love opened him up to love in a way he never thought was possible.

Another student wondered whether it was right or wrong for her to have multiple intimate relationships at the same time. Her answer to herself:

> One of my rules says no! My processmind, earth-based spot was in Central Africa, a place where the earth supports people to dance ecstatically. I learned from this earth-based viewpoint that dance is my ethics. How

did this relate to my ethical question about having more than one lover? My processmind's ethics implied, "That's natural, life is a dance." Then I realized something I had never understood before. Relationships are not my real problem! I am just not dancing enough, not only in relationships but in my life as a whole. The part of me that wanted several lovers was not right or wrong. The lovers were NOT the problem! I have not been following my deepest ethics, which was this ecstatic dance of life.

The ethics of your processmind is a dreamlike guiding wisdom that includes all your ethical values, both known and hidden. The truth is a process beyond right and wrong.

THINGS TO THINK ABOUT

1. Ethics is not just a philosophical topic but a processmind experience, the deepest meaning you attribute to your life.
2. The ethics of entangled co-creation involves evolving relationships and the compassionate wisdom of the earth-based processmind.
3. Discover and follow your own processmind's ethics.

CHAPTER 14

MYSTICISM
AND UNIFIED FIELDS

R eligion, physics, and psychology don't know yet how, when, or even if they should go together. That's one reason why addressing topics such as creation and ethics is so difficult. From a processwork viewpoint, one of the reasons for the persistent split among disciplines is the manner in which each one directs our attention. Physics, for instance, favors consensus reality and attends to repeatable measurements to define it, while considering physical theories that produce immeasurable possibilities (such as Feynman's particles going backward in time) irrelevant. Religious traditions and some psychologies, on the other hand, focus on human experience, which is largely immeasurable. The world we live in is one, but we split it into parts by focusing on either particles or dreams and ineffable feelings. From the viewpoint of this book, all these parts, particles, dreams, and ineffable feelings are aspects of the processmind.

Historically, there have been many "one world" descriptions, especially from mystics and myth makers. The Tao, described in the Tao Te Ching as "Mother of heaven and earth," and the European alchemists' Unus Mundus are two we have already considered.

A mystic, according to the Merriam Webster dictionary, senses things that "are neither apparent to the senses nor obvious to the intelligence," that is, to the rational mind. The mystic sees with eyes closed, so to speak. Mystics seek to experience unity with conscious awareness of ultimate reality or God. Mystics are often radicals, belonging to a religion while participating in practices that may lie outside it. The names they give to that experience of oneness differ according to their religion and culture.

In Christianity, mystics think of being connected to God as "illumination." In Islam this union is called *irfan*, that is, knowing the invisible; you cannot see it, but you sense it. In Buddhism, the enlightened or illuminated person has found *nirvana*, a sense of peace, an end to cravings and mental fetters. In Jainism, enlightenment is called *moksha*, meaning the end of the cycle of death and life. The Hindus see this as a state as freedom from your worldly "little you" identity, a state where matter energy, space, time, causality, and karma are no longer binding; they speak of this nondual experience as *samadhi*. The Jewish Cabala teaches that God is neither matter nor spirit but rather the oneness creator from which both emerge.

Mystics—not physicists—I believe, were the first to propose "theories of everything" because they speak about the foundations of all foundations. However, modern physics has likewise made many attempts at "theories of everything," including a unified field theory I discuss later in this chapter.

A DREAM

Before continuing, though, I must report a dream that occurred as I was beginning this chapter. In my dream I saw the last five thousand years of religious experience, both positive and negative occurrences. I saw that the strict division between groups and belief systems will now end, and in the next five thousand years people will be more connected with the essence of things. I never had a dream like that before. It obviously points to healing my own splits, but perhaps this dream is also about the future. That would mean that in the next five thousand years a more essence-based approach to spirituality and, as a result, to science will integrate consensus reality and mysticism. Processmind kinds of experiences and theories would become more important. I don't see this happening yet in the outside world, but perhaps this is a prescient dream. I surely hope so!

OMNIPRESENCE

Let's begin by considering the pervasiveness of fields. Psychologically, one of the strongest fields is a bad mood. When you are in such a field, it almost seems omnipresent, that is, present everywhere. In chapter 4 we examined presence. Our ability to perceive presence is strong; if you are on the phone with someone, only hearing her or his voice, you can still feel the person's "presence," even if she or he is on the other side of the planet. There is something "omnipresent," all or universally present, about the caller. Because of the nonlocality of entanglement, terms like *omnipresent* have become more central in science in the last thirty or forty years.

In mystical and religious systems, omnipresence has been a basic concept for a long time. The gods, especially in monotheisms, are said to be omnipresent. They are *ubiquitous*, which means "in all places." Imagine something that is present in all places *at every moment*. If something is omnipresent and also intelligent, it is omniscient, all-knowing. Omnipresence implies that its "eye" is everywhere—everything in the universe has that eye. Imagine that! This book has an eye; the tree, your friend, the light bulb has an eye; chairs have eyes; plants have eyes. The same kind of presence or awareness is everywhere.

God is sometimes described as being the same consciousness and wisdom everywhere. Does this mean that he or she is in hell as well? (The problem here is more about the point of view of the questioner than about the question itself.) Monotheistic concepts and images of God as a savior or punisher are mythic, dreamland figures. As such they are parts of the field, not the entire field. If the question is about God as the whole field, which includes all parts and all apparent opposites, then yes, at that essence level and as a kind of unified field, God is omnipresent and would be in hell as well.

I don't know how to define hell, but for me, dying on the road from a car accident, being confined to an isolation chamber in prison, and painful body experiences are all potential hells. The concept of hell presumes the existence of "absolute evil." When I was studying Jungian psychology in the 1960s, my teachers talked about, and believed in, "absolute evil." Maybe. They surely had a point. People who suffer from sociopathic or psychopathic disorders hurt others. Furthermore, some things simply are terrible, especially from the viewpoint of consensus reality. Nevertheless, I prefer to keep an open mind about evil's absolute nature. I have worked with killers, Nazi SS officers, and other people who committed dreadful crimes. Yet even in the midst of the horrible details of their stories, often there was still a redeeming "presence" or evidence of processmind essence. As a result, for me, there is no absolute evil—except for a short period of time and from one viewpoint.

The question of good and evil reminds me of a painful scene Amy and I worked with during a conflict-resolution situation in South Africa before the revolution.[1] A woman said to someone else, in the middle of the conflict work, "I want to kill you." She would kill the other person at the end of this meeting if they could not come to an agreement. "I will stab you to death with the knife in my pocket." Another participant, who had been spared a life of conflict and poverty, naively said to the potential aggressor, "No, you don't really want to do that, no, you don't." When I pressed the potential knife holder to go more deeply into her anger, she said that she was saying these things because she was desperate and felt that "this is my last chance to work things out!" If she and her people could not get what they needed, she would "just as well kill and be killed." That is hopelessness, not evil. Belief in the omnipresence of the story maker makes it possible to go deeper, beneath the surface events and feelings. What looks like evil at the surface may not be evil from a more unified or encompassing viewpoint.

A TOE and a Grand Foot

Let's look more closely at the physicists' attempt at an all-encompassing "theory of everything," or TOE.[2] Physicists are interested in a TOE because they need a theory connecting quantum theory to relativity. They are hoping for unifications. In this same sense, mysticism is a TOE, a sense that some grand intelligence or pattern lies behind everything.

Physicists call one particular TOE the grand unified field theory. According to the prevailing measurements and view of the universe, it was created with a "Big Bang" about 13.7 billion years ago, resulting in an expanding universe with vast spaces and spiraling galaxies. Einstein's relativity theory, which deals with the curved space-time of the vast outer universe, explains that gravity tries to hold those galaxies and everything else together.[3] Quantum mechanics, on the other hand, deals with the realm of particles you can't quite see, where time is reversible. Relativity theory and quantum theory are vastly different and do not agree upon the very nature of space itself. The space-time curvature of the visible universe does not work well in the quantum realm because space-time is a continuum, like a huge rubber mattress, whereas the spaces of the quantum realm are more like bits of rubber the size of a grain of sand. This difference is one reason why there is a problem bringing relativity and quantum theory together.

Physicists do not yet know how to unify the grand spaces of the universe and their gravity field with the tiny, particle-like spaces of quantum theory and their quantum-range forces. Attempts to create a grand unified field theory are based on force-field concepts. They try to bring relativity and quantum theory together by unifying the four known force fields: gravity, electromagnetism, and the strong and weak nuclear forces.

As a therapist, I suggest there can be no TOE or grand unified field theory without including psychology and spirituality. We can't call it a theory of "everything" if it doesn't include people, dreams, and feelings!

The prospect of unifying physics and psychology has fascinated many people. I think of Jung and his work with the Nobel prize-winning physicist Wolfgang Pauli. (See Jung's work on synchronicity in volume 8 of his *Collected Works*, where he speaks about the Unus Mundus, the one world of the alchemists.) Perhaps what we need is a diverse TOE, a theory of everything that relates to all disciplines. Better yet, maybe we need not one TOE but many—five or ten or more to stand on! To "under-stand" everything and also connect to the earth, we need a "foot"! Each TOE would be different, yet the essence of each would connect them all and be different from any of them, just as the foot is different from any single toe. We need a Grand Foot, not just a TOE.[4]

According to today's physics, everyday reality consists of space, time, and objects. Inside the objects are different types of particles, such as electrons and protons and neutrons. And in between these particles are fields. No one really knows exactly what a field is, but in the standard model of quantum physics, the enigma of fields is explained by the the-ory of exchange particles.

Let me explain. The measurable forces of a field (such as an electro-magnetic field) between oppositely charged particles are imagined to be created by the movement of virtual particles, or photons. Particle physi-cists imagine that the virtual particles, like tiny balls, are bouncing back and forth between negative and positive figures or charged particles, creating the push and pull we call electromagnetic force. In figure 14.1, "Virtual Particle Exchange," two people (representing charged particles)

Figure 14.1. Virtual Particle Exchange.

are shown throwing a ball back and forth. You could think of one person as being negatively charged, the other as positive. The ball is meant to represent a virtual particle that pushes the charged particles apart, creating an electromagnetic field between them.

Virtual particles correspond in many ways to psychological experiences. The pull and push between people in relationships can be noticed as tiny flirts and signals, feedback, and discussions. Flirts are experienced as little *pings*—that is, like exchange particles. You get little pings, and then you ask yourself and others, "How does that strike you?" Apparently we are "struck" by flirts. You can't see the virtual photons, and you also can't see the flirts in the moment they occur—at least not easily.

The Four Physical Forces

In today's physics there are four known forces or force fields (with associated virtual particles). Let's look at them one at a time and take a guess at the psychological experiences, analogies, and metaphors that might be connected to or even behind our understanding of these physical fields.

Electromagnetism. The electromagnetic field is what makes it possible for a magnet to lift a metal clip off a table. This field corresponds to the everyday sense of attraction or repulsion that is preceded by flirts. You feel drawn or repelled by certain kinds of people when there are enough flirts moving between you!

The strong force. The nucleus of an atom consists of protons, which are positively charged, and neutrons, which have no charge. What force holds those positively charged protons together and stops them from repelling one another? Today this force is called the "strong force." Its presence is short-ranged, only extending within the tiny nucleus, but it is so powerful that if you interrupt the strong force of the nucleus, you release atomic energy. We should all know about the strong force. Today it is a major political force!—a matter of life, death, and politics for all of us on our little planet.

An analogy of the strong force in psychology is the force holding our center together, our nucleus, our personal myth. Inside your processmind, the "strong force" holds together things that you would normally expect to repel one another. Personal myths are "nuclear" cores. Connect to that and you find the energy and passion of a lifetime. If you deny that core, you get depressed because of lack of energy. The strong force of our personal myth or organizational center can bring us to life. Likewise, connect to the core nature of another person and you create an almost unbreakable bond. That is why "breaking up" is so explosive! The mythic power at the nucleus of relationships and organizations can be amazingly creative or destructive.

The weak force. The weak force, also a nuclear force, gets its name by being 10^{13} times less strong than the strong force. It is not as well understood as the strong force. Its best-known effect is radioactivity, or the beta decay of electrons in an unstable nucleus. The weak force reminds me of the little *puff* that is enough to set off an avalanche when the snow is almost hanging off a cliff.

Psychological versions of the weak force occur when you are in an unstable situation. For example, when you feel "edgy," a little *puff* can make you feel crazy and set off "avalanches" around you. If you were already moody, one (weak little) wrong look from someone can create a catastrophe! On the other hand, if you are in a quiet, processmind state, that little force can release sudden radiance and creativity. In deep meditation, a tiny almost-nothing something can produce new creative ideas.

Zen calligraphers work with this kind of "weak force." They sit in the "no mind" or *mu-shin* state and then suddenly pick up their brush and produce beautiful calligraphy. My friend the calligrapher Fukushima Roshi works this way: first he meditates, and then he lets his Zen mind (or what he calls his creative mind) create.

The Tao can also be a "weak force." According to the Tao Te Ching, the Tao is "nothing." It is very small. *Wu-wei*, or "not-doing," means following the Tao by taking effortless action. A little flirt sets off an incredible radiance and, if you follow it, you become almost "radioactive."

Gravity. Gravity is very different from the other three force fields. Relativity theory explains that gravity comes from the many different ways in which space-time can bend and twist. If you are sitting on a bare mattress, without blankets or sheets, and drop a ball on it, chances are the ball will roll toward the most indented part of the mattress where you are seated. According to Einstein, the space-time curvature of our universe is indented like that mattress, and the resulting curvature makes things roll in certain ways. What we experience as the earth's gravity is, from the viewpoint of relativity, linked to the space-time curvature around the earth.

Most people don't think about gravity much unless they are astronauts or are worried about their weight and must stand on a scale. Perhaps the first and last fight we will ever have is with gravity, and we can never win. The material part of us always goes back to the earth.

Gravity organizes and seems to hold the entire universe together; it glues galaxies together, and it even holds particles to one another. However, because gravity is so incredibly weak, the weakest of the forces, all you need is just a little bar magnet to lift a paper clip off your desktop. Being the subtlest of all the forces, gravity is that "almost nothing" that gives us a pull here or there, that makes us feel heavy. Yet in spite of its subtle nature, it has an infinite range (like the electromagnetic force); it affects things at the other end of the universe and holds us together.

In psychology, gravity corresponds to the Dreaming, to the subtle sense of the earth, to the common-ground feeling, and to the sense that everything attracts everything else, even things that we think should be opposites.

In many ways, the processmind is very close to the nature of gravity. For example, like gravity, the processmind has (feeling-wise) an infinite range. The processmind subtle force can seem at one moment simultaneously very close and also very far from our awareness. When we see leaders motivated by something compassionate and deep within themselves, we can be moved as if by gravity. It is all-inclusive and apparently attracts all matter, all figures, and doesn't tend to polarize. Rather, it embraces all its parts and vectors. Today, it's the only field without a known virtual particle, though the speculated "graviton" is being sought. In our present degree of knowledge, gravity is the one field that is identical to the bending of space-time. It is due to, or coincident with, the shape of the universe, the home in which we live. It is analogous to the "atmosphere" or "aura" of our grandest beliefs as well as our near-death and nonlocal experiences.

PSYCHOLOGICAL AND PHYSICAL FIELD CONNECTIONS

Force fields are basic not only to physics but to psychology as well. Sigmund Freud talked about drives or instincts, Alfred Adler about power, Jung about complexes. Because Freud seems to have borrowed the term *complex* from chemistry, complexes and drives in psychology are indirectly linked to electrostatic chemistry fields and forces.[5] Some of the TOEs in psychology might go by terms such as the *subconscious*, the *unconscious*, the *Self*, *gestalt*, or even *process*. After all, they are all "field-like" and can be experienced as exerting force at a distance.

Because of the analogies between the forces and fields of psychology and physics, I must ask if these disciplines can be brought together with a new TOE, TOEs, or even a Grand Foot? The processmind could be such a single field that unifies the psychological and physical force fields and includes spirituality as well. Like the four forces of physics, the processmind often appears at first as a subtle feeling that cannot be verbalized; it is a feeling sense without parts. It's like gravity in that it seems to embrace everything. As it arises closer to our everyday mind, it appears as flirts in dreamland—like the exchange particles of physics. It appears as the passion and power of our core, "nuclear" myth, and in consensus reality as opposites (such as "good" or "evil") that attract and repel us, comparable to electrostatic opposites. It seems to have a presence, an omnipresence, in fact, and an intelligence. It can't be seen, but it can surely be felt. That is why the Taoists spoke about it in terms of wavelike dragon lines in the earth. Three-thousand-year-old Taoist "wave" diagrams are reminiscent of today's field concepts (see chapter 5).

We don't know what created the processmind any more than we know the origins of the universe's physical fields. But it sometimes seems as if the processmind is the creator, or co-creator, of everything else. If the processmind is like the Tao, then it has been present since before the beginning, as the mother of heaven and earth.

It is difficult but important to try to describe TOEs such as the processmind; our world needs them. We need new ideas that explain why our awareness steadily oscillates between sleeping, dreaming, and waking. We need a Grand Foot to "under-stand" more about creation and co-creation in the physical, psychological, and spiritual senses and reconnect us to our Aboriginal roots. We need to explore what many scientists such as Einstein speculate is the "mind of God." The future will reveal how the processmind is linked to the origin of consciousness and our experience of the origin of life.

The following exercise addresses possible questions about the Grand Foot and about unified field theories by giving you your own experience of how TOEs arise. If you are shy about prolonged altered states, just read this exercise, for it requires, to some extent, a prolonged immersion in the processmind state.

EXERCISE 14: THE UNIFIED FIELD THEORY IN LIFE

To begin, make a note about any problems bothering you recently. Also note any "big" questions you want to think about just now.

After you write down your questions, once again scan your body to locate the deepest part of yourself. Breathe into that area, taking your time. Deepen that body experience by focusing your breath on that area. When you are ready, try to associate this experience with some earth spot. Go to that place on earth and see it. Then when you are ready, become this spot itself. Be that earth spot, be the earth meditating. Take your time. Perhaps you will feel the spot's presence or notice its power. Look around and feel the presence of this spot not just where you are but all around this area. In what way are you this area's field presence—whatever that means to you? Can you get a glimpse of what it might be like to be a nonlocal, omnipresent force field?

If you are able to remain in that processmind experience, continue meditating until something pops up on its own, until something that seems "important" occurs to you. Write down a note about it under #14 on the collage page.

How do you describe the nature of your processmind's field? What physical, spiritual, or other terms do you use to describe this part of your nature? Is it a strong force, a subtle experience? Does it have sounds or colors or motions? Ask your processmind where its intelligence comes from, if anywhere. Could you sense your processmind as a subtle gravity, "pulling" on things? Is it a real or dreamlike? Is it a unifying field in any sense? If so, in what sense?

Now think about the questions you posed at the beginning of this exercise. Perhaps your processmind will give you some answers. Ask how this processmind experience can possibly be of use throughout your personal life.

THE POWER OF HAWAII

During a class I gave on field theories, I worked with a very shy student who was troubled about how to share her feelings with others. She had just completed the preceding exercise and wanted to go further to work on her shyness in public.

She found her deepest self located in her heart area. After breathing into that body area, she felt herself in Hawaii, right on a beach on Maui. Here is her verbatim description of the experience.

There is something very friendly, warm, and spacious in that Maui beach area. It has a different sense than the ocean. Some oceans can be foreboding, but this has a vast, open, come-join-me kind of feeling. I feel I am right down there on the beach. . . . It is beautiful . . . the field there is something very inviting, fluid and warm, and also something very relaxed. [While standing on her feet, she began to rock from side to side.]

[Laughing] I am rarely actually like this. It becomes vast and expansive and has a gentle, sweet power that goes and goes and goes . . . it makes me dance and radiate . . . it is neither inside, nor outside but . . . both!

Ah-ha! I got it! This dance that is being neither inside nor outside is how to share my feelings . . . wow . . . it is so altering and wonderful. Yes, it is subtle and yet very powerful. . . . Is it intelligence? It is just there, was always there, before anything else was here.

That Maui beach is her personal "unified field theory," an omnipresence connecting various aspects of her life. Months later, I asked this student if this work had had any effect on her shyness. She said, "I return in my memory to this Maui experience many times, and it makes everything I do in public much easier and more awesome."

THINGS TO THINK ABOUT

1. At this time, there are four known forces in physics and many instincts, drives, and forces in psychology.
2. The processmind may emerge into consensus reality in the form of the different kinds of fields in physics and psychology.
3. Whether or not processmind is a unified field theory, having a conscious, personal sense of this field can make life "more awesome" and give us a "foot," not just a toe, to stand on.

PART FOUR

NONLOCALITY AND THE ENTANGLEMENT DANCE

I believe in intuition and inspiration.
Imagination is more important than knowledge.
For knowledge is limited, whereas imagination
embraces the entire world, stimulating progress,
giving birth to evolution. It is, strictly speaking,
a real factor in scientific research.

— Albert Einstein, *Cosmic Religion*

ENTANGLEMENT IN RELIGION, PHYSICS, AND PSYCHOLOGY

Researchers, mystics, and all those interested in facilitating the creation of a better world need many different keys to the future. The key I am stressing in this book is to maintain awareness of your deepest self while you are working and playing in everyday reality. By relating to your depths, you gain better understanding of others and remain closer to your own ethics, however you formulate them.

Being half in your own depths and half out can transform your experience of reality as well. When you are close to the "unified field" experiences of the processmind, experiences in psychology, physics, and spirituality overlap in a way that sometimes makes it difficult to rationally understand or even cognitively follow the course of events. Yet, the unifying effects of being close to your basic "force field" become very real in the way you connect with yourself and others even during very difficult times. In this last section, part four, I want to explore the magical and creative effects of being "half in, half out." I will go more deeply into the nonlocality, entanglement, and structures of "god processes" to help show how a slight shift in identity can reveal magical elements of everyday life.

I remember one day saying to Amy, who is, among other things, an artist, "I want to talk about this quantum thing called entanglement." When I described what I meant, she said, "Well, of course! I have always known all about that!" Her comment did me a lot of good. I had forgotten that what science is discovering is, in some sense, what sensitive people have always known. Entanglement is easily experienced by shamans, but explaining it in everyday-reality language is a challenge. To begin with, let's see how entanglement might fit with concepts of God.

The Structure of God Experiences

Let's begin with spiritual traditions, with the great "entanglers"—the gods in mystical and religious traditions. To make things simple, I'll limit this discussion to ideas about God in the three main monotheistic traditions: Judaism, Christianity, and Islam, although what I say is general enough to fit most traditions. In brief, in these traditions, God processes have at least the following four attributes: omniscience, omnipresence, omnipotence, and flow.[1]

Omniscience. Omniscience, or all-knowingness, implies infinite awareness and universal knowledge. I don't think the processmind is all-knowing, but it is consistently intelligent, at least regarding the next steps for you, for other individuals, and for relationships and organizations. You may have experienced some form of "omniscience" in the exercises of previous chapters.

Omnipresence. Omnipresence means being present in all places and times, as we saw in the previous chapter. When you are in touch with your processmind, it feels like you can connect to almost anyone or anything anywhere. In fact, trying to locate your processmind in just one single point in space and time often seems to miss the point! The processmind is a presence that is omnipresent at least in the limited sense that it has no spatial or temporal boundaries. The processmind's omnipresence can be felt in relationships. For example, even though you and your friend live on opposite sides of the planet, you sometimes feel as if there were no distance between you. We call this friendship *love* and think of it as "magic." However, when the relationship is troubled, we say that there is a "great distance" between us. Omnipresence in friendship is the sense of being part of a distanceless oneness, the quality described in physics as nonlocality.

Omnipotence. Human beings are not omnipotent, that is, all-powerful. But when you are close to the processmind, it surely feels like some all-knowing, all-present power is moving you to have amazing insights. I don't think the everyday part of your mind has that power, though many have said that they "make" that power "happen." Process-mind power comes from an altered state: It is simply there in nature. It supports but does not follow the wishes of your "little you"; it seems to guide the overall nature of your feelings and dreams. For example, the processmind's presence may give you a momentary sense of energy or "power," guidance and wellness, that sometimes seems to be more important than life itself.

Flow. Change, movement, and process are characteristic of all creation myths. In many sacred myths, flow appears in fluid symbols such as water. For example, Genesis 1:2–5 says that, in the beginning, the earth was formless and void, and darkness was over the surface of the deep, and the Spirit of God was hovering over the surface of the waters. It seems to me that these waters refer to the depth and fluidity of the processmind as it is experienced at the essence level, before wisdom, personified in the myth as the face of the creator, occurs. Water also plays a central role in Islamic tradition. *Sharia*, the term for the body of Islamic religious law, means "path to the water source."

My point is that the processmind is partially mirrored in the flow structures of "god processes," that is, in terms of omnipresence, omni-science, omnipotence, and flow, or in some entangled sum of all these characteristics. These characteristics are usually mixed together in an undifferentiated form we simply identify as processmind experience. In the exercises in this book, you may have had emotional, earth-based experiences that contain one or all four of these characteristics.

Entanglement. I now want to now add entanglement, a fifth characteristic to the other four God processes, to bring spiritual traditions and physics closer. The first four characteristics can be linked to religious and spiritual traditions. However, I can best describe entanglement in terms of physics. In chapter 7, under the topic of the "deep democracy" of relationships, I pointed out that in quantum physics, if two particles emerged from the same quantum source, they remain entangled and can no longer be considered separately. This means that if you observe one, you know what the other is doing—without looking at it. This sounds reasonable if the two particles are right next to one another within a quantum system such as a well-insulated, small box. But what if these two particles end up at different ends of the planet or the universe? The fact that, according to physics, they remain entangled borders on magic. That is why before entanglement was demonstrated in the laboratory, Einstein was skeptical about quantum entanglement, saying that it "sounds like spooky action at a distance!"[2] But quantum entanglement is an empirical fact. As long as the quantum system is not disturbed—that is, as long as the particles remain connected to the same quantum system—whatever happens to one connects to the other, no matter the physical distance.

In principle, if the entire universe emerged from the Big Bang, then everything is part of one quantum system. For this reason, some scientists suggest that every material object must be entangled with everything else in some way or other. Since it's not (yet) possible to do an experiment involving the entire universe, universal entanglement remains a speculation. However, most shamans would have no problem with the concept. For them, telepathy, precognition, remote viewing, and all sorts of thought and energy transfers are not speculations but realities.

QUANTUM NONLOCALITY

Entanglement was first intuited, as far as I know, in 1935 by Erwin Schrödinger, one of the parents of quantum theory. He predicted that particles could connect with one another nonlocally, which means at speeds apparently faster than the speed of light. In the equations involving isolated quantum systems, he saw the possibility that two particles, such as A and B, that were originally connected will always be so, even if they travel to opposite sides of the world. In other words, if A and B were originally together in a quantum system, at a later date if you know what A is doing, you know what B is doing even if you cannot see B yourself. Just looking at A lets you know what B is doing even if B is on the moon! Are they sending signals faster than the speed of light to one another? No. That would violate relativity theory. Then how do they remain connected? No one knows.

Why did Einstein think that this quantum phenomenon was spooky? Perhaps he was afraid of magic. In my mind, science and spiritual traditions, which for centuries had been married, tried to get divorced in the seventeenth century as classical physics arose. Once a couple is divorced, they don't often like seeing each other much. But now, in the twenty-first century, here comes religion, back in the form of something like omnipresence, in the midst of quantum physics. Because of entanglement, science and religion are back in each other's faces! The conflict facilitator in me predicts that after about four hundred years of divorce, science and religion may be headed for a remarriage through ideas such as the processmind. It could be one of the matchmakers.

The entanglement cartoon in figure 15.1 depicts some of the details of the physics of entanglement. Think of a quantum system as a box with two particles, A and B. Let's represent what A and B are doing by arrows that go up or down. Those arrows represent what scientists call the *spin* of a particle. *Spin* is a mathematical concept signifying the angular momentum of an elementary particle. To understand spin, remember that a spinning top continues to spin because of its momentum, or indwelling force. (To get a psychological sense of spin, think of it as imagination. To "spin" is to dream. When you have a new idea, or a new "spin" on something, you have momentum. If you think one thing, your friend may have a different "spin" on the same thing. Dreaming

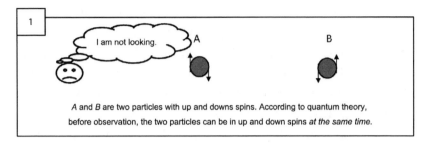

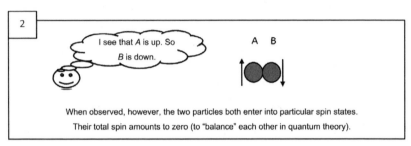

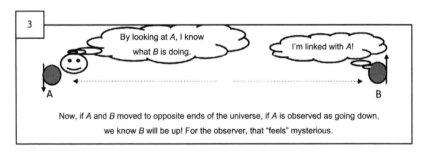

Figure 15.1. Entanglement Cartoon.

has its own momentum. Some dreams are "uppers," whereas others are "downers.")

Physicists represent spin by up and down arrows. In the first cartoon strip, since the particles are not being observed, they can be in two states at the same time, that is, spinning both up and down. How can something be in two states at the same time? That's one of the characteristics of superposition. As we saw in chapter 3, Schrödinger's cat was both dead and alive—until it was observed. That's the quantum world! In the second cartoon strip, if the overall state of the enclosed system has zero spin, then the particles must spin in opposite directions, one up and one down. In the third cartoon strip, A and B are separated but since they are still parts of the same system, they maintain their entanglement. Thus, you know what B is doing simply by looking at A.

Entanglement phenomena point to a spaceless interconnected realm spanned by the quantum system pattern, the quantum wave equation. In other words, when we measure the spin of one particle, we are measuring the spin arrangement of the *entire* system that is operating as a unit.

In my mind, both Einstein and Schrödinger were right. Reality *is* spooky! Yet reality exists and is organized, to some extent, by the equations of physics behind entanglement. That is why physicists say that the quantum realm is counter-intuitive. It's weird. What binds the entangled particles together? Is it the Holy Ghost? Links in the quantum world do not operate via visible signals you can track with a video camera. No. In fact, A does *not* send any known signal to B. Their connection is more like an altered state of oscillating oneness that also recognizes everyday reality: that is, half in and half out.

How can one particle be connected with another without any signals going between them? How do you sometimes know something without any visible message or transfer of information? Without a smoke signal, telephone call, email, or TV connection, how do you occasionally know when someone close to you has trouble, or dies, or experiences some great luck? Physics has no complete answer and simply calls this space-defying connection "nonlocality."

Guessing what is behind nonlocality, Nobel Prize-winning physicist David Bohm spoke of the universe in terms of its "undivided wholeness." More recently, Amit Goswami has spoken of monism and "consciousness" as the prime reality from which everything else is derived.[3] Others say these ideas are too speculative because they can't be tested. Regardless of how entanglement is viewed, it is here to stay. In fact, a whole new breed of quantum computers may soon be based upon entanglement: instead of being based on a binary system in which each bit of information must be either 0 or 1, quantum machines will have "qubits" of information that can be 0, 1, or a mixture (superposition) of both.

THE PROCESSMIND'S "BODY"

Let me try to explain the unexplainable entanglement phenomena by means of pictures and Erwin Schrödinger's words. Take a look at figure 15.2, a NASA artist's representation of entanglement between particles *A* and *B*. At the bottom of the picture, the artist imagines a platform with a crystal on it. Below the crystal is a beam that rises up and strikes the crystal, emitting two photons, *A* and *B*, that emerge into the sky. Now if you were able to measure photon *A*'s state with a satellite, you would know *B*'s state regardless of how far A and B are from one another. How can that be? The artist simply paints a horizontal wave ~~~~~~ connecting *A* and *B*.

Figure 15.2. NASA Artist's Depiction of Entanglement.

The mystery remains, what is that wave? In this book, I have tried to demonstrate my guess; that wave is meant to represent a body feeling I call the processmind! Here is how I came to that conclusion.

Erwin Schrödinger was living in England when he first came up with the entanglement idea. Being originally from Austria, he used the German word for entanglement, *verschraenkung*, which also means "crossing" or "folding." This German word is normally used for describing crossed legs. This fact makes me think that perhaps he was thinking of two feet, *A* and *B*, being crossed even while describing the "crossing" of two particles, *A* and *B* (see figure 15.3).

In figure 15.4 the feet are also crossed, but if you did not know that those feet belonged to someone's body, you might wonder how foot *A* would know how to relate to foot *B*, especially if the two feet were on the opposite sides of the universe! These two feet are all we see in the lab. It is only in your heart or subtle-body sensations that you can sense such a "body" or intelligence or, as David Bohm put it, "undivided wholeness" behind things. My guess is that Schrödinger was thinking of entanglement as a connection through some sort of organizing intelligence in the background, just as two crossed arms or feet are connected through a body. Physicists today call that "body" simply "nonlocality."

Figure 15.3. Crossed Legs.

Figure 15.4.
Crossed Legs—Just the Feet.

CHAPTER 15

ENTANGLEMENT FROM THE PROCESSMIND'S VIEWPOINT

At the essence level, the processmind encompasses various sides of itself, or compositions (superpositions) of its various sides. When we focus only on one part of this unity, some of the unitive experience is lost, just as a quantum wave holding multiple possibilities collapses into a single upon observation. In the 1950s, Jung noted in his paper on "Synchronicity" (in volume 8 of his *Collected Works*) that when even the average person is deeply involved in an event or process, synchronicities seem to occur regularly; otherwise, they occur less frequently. In other words, the omniscient, omnipotent, omnipresent, entangled flow of the processmind is most often accessed when we are connected with its altered state.

In exercises in earlier chapters you may have felt how the processmind's earth-based area entangles your experiences and its parts. The trees and distant mountains, the sky above and the earth below, the water and the rocks on the beach are interconnected, "entangled," by the power of the land. This, I believe, is what Uncle Lewis was referring to when he spoke of the Red Kangaroo Dreaming behind the streets of Adelaide (see chapter 10). Totem spirits are the land's power (analogous to the quantum wave function), and they organize everything in the city, including acting on the very development of the road system of that city. From this viewpoint, everything in the city is, in principle, entangled with everything else.

The fact that the processmind is a unity encompassing many various experiences is illustrated in figure 15.5. If you focus long enough on the figure at the bottom, you can probably perceive how it contains both the duck and the rabbit figures, shown separately above it. The point is not just seeing the duck and rabbit in the single drawing but noticing how the mind flips back and forth between them. This is analogous to the way the processmind works. When you are in your processmind, it seems to swing from one part of itself to another, with little or no separation between the parts. This is what psychological nonlocality is all about: the sense of closeness among parts, particles, people, and objects that in everyday reality seem separate in every possible manner.

Figure 15.5. Processmind Superposition. The duck-rabbit superposition appears in consensus reality as a duck and a rabbit.

Moreover, if you focus on the consensus reality view of the rabbit, because of entanglement you will always know approximately what the duck is doing, and vice versa. Why? Because they are really phases of one system. For example, imagine that the duck has a closed mouth; the rabbit's ears will be closed, too. Entanglement! But if you get out of contact with the duck-rabbit essence level, then consensus reality appears, and every-thing—here, the duck and rabbit—appear separate and independent.

EXERCISE 15: ENTANGLED FLIRTS

The best understanding of entanglement may come from your own experience. In principle, everything that "flirts" with your attention is the processmind appearing in diverse forms. If you are the duck, the rabbit catches your attention, and vice versa. We call that flirt a flickering (mental) image or a dream, and we take it as being meaningful for our personal psychology. But from another viewpoint, it is an attempt on the part of our processmind to show us the whole system, to balance the different spins.

Let's try the exercise. Once again, standing is best, but sitting is okay, too. Take your collage pages and pen with you. Close your eyes and relax. Feel your body, notice your breathing. Wait until you notice the feeling of being breathed. That is important because it gets you out of your everyday mind. Give yourself time to drop into an altered state. When you are ready, slowly let your eyes open halfway while you remain in a kind of foggy state. Let your eyes drift or gaze around you, and let something, one thing, catch your attention. Many things may catch your attention. If you don't know which thing to choose, let your unconscious mind, your processmind, choose.

Look at the one thing that caught your attention. See it, per-haps become it a bit, and sense/know it as a part of you needed in the moment. Then let your processmind tell you which part of you needed to see that flirt. Who is the observer inside of you that needed to see it? Make a note on the collage page, in one corner of square #15, about these two parts: the flirt and the observer of that flirt. Sense and sketch both their energies quickly on paper.

Now take a moment, relax, and feel yourself being breathed again. When you are ready, sense the intelligence in you that knows you as the observer and also knows the thing that caught your attention. In other words, look at the observer and the flirt that caught your attention and ask: "What sort of totem spirit or earth-based intelligence knew how to bring that flirt to me?" This is an intuitive experience; just trust your experience and quick insights.

Once you know that spirit, when you're ready, shift identities and sense yourself as that spirit, as the processmind intelligence that knew your everyday self and what was needed at a given moment. Again, trust your intuition and feeling about whatever that processmind intelligence might be. When you have a sense of it, talk to yourself as that processmind and describe your processmind's wisdom, intelligence, and nature. Make a note about this. When you are ready, let the processmind use your hand to draw itself in some way on the collage page in square #15. Write down any words it said.

Now, sense and be your processmind intelligence and be that sketch. Move your awareness back and forth from the representation of the flirt that caught your attention to the representation of the part of you who needed to see that flirt. Move back and forth between the two until you sense how both are somehow aspects of the same processmind source. Make a note, if you like.

Finally, consider these questions: Has this flirt been trying to reach your attention as a body feeling, a dream, or in other ways in the past days? Have you been in conflict with the part of life represented by that flirt? Can you sense how that flirt and you, as the observer, are entangled? Imagine now that if *you* change the flirt might change as well. You can test this idea, for you *have* changed a bit because of this exercise. So go through the exercise once again to see what catches your attention now. Note this second experience: The original flirt may have changed in connection with your change. That is entanglement!

MY SYNCHRONICITY EXPERIENCE

As part of a presentation at a seminar on the coast, I gave an explanation of entanglement, and then, with Amy's help, went through the above exercise. When I relaxed and felt as if I were being breathed, the flirt that caught my attention was an electric ceiling fan spinning on the ceiling of the seminar room. In my inner experience, I realized

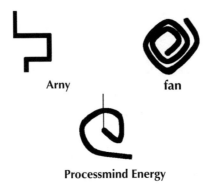

Arny   **fan**

Processmind Energy

Figure 15.6. Processmind Energy Sketch. Here processmind energy combines two energies, the linear Arny and the circular fan.

that the part of me who needed to see that spinning fan was the linear teacher in me. As I worked through the exercise, I could feel how the two parts—the linear me, and the spinning fan—were entangled. See my processmind energy sketch (see figure 15.6).

At the moment I realized the meaning of the fan, I did a little bow in its direction to honor it for showing me how to be a "spinning" teacher; and right then and there, in the midst of all those people, the fan "spoke" to me! I mean, the fan began to make weird squeaky sounds as it went around and around. A fan making weird sounds like that has *never* happened before to me, in the many years I have taught in that room! Nor has such an event ever happened to me anywhere. Entanglement! My processmind was like a river embracing and linking my linear self and the fan—that is, the linear teacher and my relaxed, dizzy, spinning mind. While in that altered state of mind, I could feel how that fan and my linear self were both entangled parts of my nonlocal processmind. In that room with that group of people, as long as I was in the processmind state, the synchronicity seemed almost "normal," that is, reasonable. My larger processmind's nonlocal body included not only my everyday body but the fan as well.

Only later, after I came out of that state, did I realize, "This is amazing!" From my normal viewpoint, something amazing had happened.

But from the processmind viewpoint, the "everyday me" and the flirt are simply entangled dreamland roles or parts of the processmind. The fan had to "speak" so that I could learn to spin.

Perhaps if I spin more, the fan will need to speak less? In any case, one entanglement lesson for the "everyday you" is that to identify a human being as only one body in one state is unnecessarily restrictive—a marginalization and thus an insult to his or her processmind—even if it is conventional. We are, of course, our everyday self, but our nonlocal entangled processmind's body also includes the flirt and the magical spaces among all physical objects, images, parts, and states.

THINGS TO THINK ABOUT

1. Entanglement is structured in physics by the math of the quantum wave function.
2. In religion, entanglement is due to God's omniscient, omnipresent, omnipotent flow that entangles everything and everyone.
3. To have a more magical life, stay half in the processmind's earth-based experience, which entangles everything and everyone that flirts with you.
4. If something catches your attention, become it in order to participate as a conscious observer in the universe's "mind of God."

ENTANGLEMENT
AS A SOFTSKILL IN
RELATIONSHIPS

From the consensus reality viewpoint, your relationships are created by your everyday self and other people. The viewpoint of the processmind is different. Relationships between people begin as a sensation or interest that occurs before those involved realize it consciously. The people and objects that flirt with your attention just happen to you, as if they were a puppet with an ever-changing face. Behind that flirting puppet face is the processmind, which, like a puppeteer, organizes what you notice. In figure 16.1, I sketched both the things like X that flirt with you and also the part of you that needs to see that flirt, "u" (which is also a puppet!).

Like the puppet on a stick held by that puppeteer, the world around you—the amazing things you see, your viewpoints, your everyday reality and friends—all these things are entangled and rooted in the processmind. The origins of our consciousness and perhaps of life itself appear in the form of X flirting with u, who is needing to see that X. Life is the processmind's wonder about itself and its tendency to self-reflect through u looking at X. Flirts are the processmind's self-reflection entangled with u; they point to the essence of the life process as a relationship.

The purpose of this chapter is to explore the processmind's softskill as seen in the puppet theater. The relationship ability or softskill behind the puppet show is what I call "quantum theater." This softskill is the

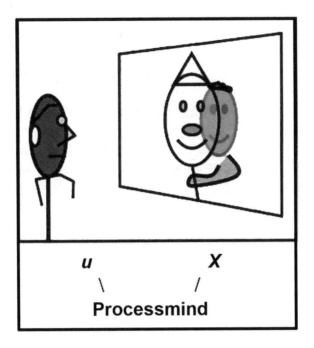

Figure 16.1. The Processmind's Puppets, $u + X$.

tendency in everyone to seek the processmind of a situation and use it to choreograph the movements of u and X in relationship. This choreography is a key to the mystery of our interconnections with others and to working with relationships and world issues.

HYDROGEN AND ITS MOLECULE

In chapter 15, we saw, in the NASA illustration of entanglement, how photons beamed at a crystal releases two entangled photons from that crystal. Now let's look at another physical example of entanglement that may seem closer to the subject of human relationships. Consider the chemical element hydrogen. One of the earliest elements of our universe, hydrogen is imagined as a positively charged nucleus with a negatively charged electron in its shell (see figure 16.2).

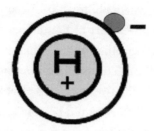

Figure 16.2. Hydrogen Atom.

When two hydrogen atoms join, they share electrons, forming what is called a "covalent bond." (See the top part of figure 16.3.) Curious physicists have wondered about that molecule. As long as the molecule is intact, it seems reasonable to assume that the electrons are entangled because they are so close to one another—if you know what one is doing, you know what the other is doing.

Intact covalent hydrogen molecule. Electrons are the negatively charged black balls.	
After photon bombardment, the bond between the A and B electrons loosens, but they are still entangled.	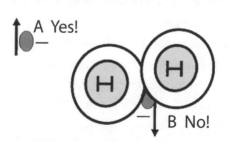

Figure 16.3. H-H Bond Entanglement.

But what happens when photons are beamed at the molecule to loosen that bond? The lower part of figure 16.3 shows one electron, A, moving away to the left. In other words, when hydrogen is bombarded by a laser beam, one of the electrons flies off in a new direction. However, as you may have guessed, the two separated electrons remain entangled. Someone observing electron A would be able to predict what someone else would see observing electron B, even if the two are far apart.

Hydrogen is a chemical fact, and it is also a metaphor of what happens to us in relationship. One atom and its electron is you, and the other atom and electron is a friend of yours. The electrons are the flirts and shared dreams that float between the two of you, holding you together in the relationship. These flirts are what attract each of you to the other and keep both of you "balanced" and in connection.

Using this chemical analogy, relationship is a quantum system, a molecule you share with anyone to whom you feel bonded. Your dreamlike experiences are like entangled electrons. As a result of this entanglement, dreams and flirts become nonlocal. Likewise, in terms of u and X, where X can be something about your friend that is on your mind or catches your attention, you are both u and X. Your $u + X$ experiences are specific to you, of course, but at the same time they are nonlocal, shared experiences that help bond you to your friend. In this sense, both u and X are flirt-like and nonlocal; they are entangled and connected with your friend, even if your friend is not in bed with you but on the other side of the globe.

For example, Amy's curly hair flirts with me. I love her hair. The linear part of me, u, needs to see her curly hair, which for me is an X. However, the energy of that "curly mind" and the u or energy of my "linear mind" are nonlocal. How? Amy has the same dyad within her: the curly and the linear. And in our relationship, when she is in a curly mindset, I am more linear, and when I am curly, she gets linear. This happens when we are next to one another and also when we are in different cities. This u-X entanglement is a synchronistic process. What is synchronous and nonlocal is the dyad, the tangle between the curly and linear minds, the way in which the u and X flip-flop, like the spins of entangled particles.

By this model, our thoughts and feelings belong to us as individuals, yet, at the same time, they may be entangled with the thoughts and feelings of our friends and all the people we know. From the perspective of the relationship's processmind, there is just one dreaming process happening with two channels of expression: you and me. Among all the things we can share with another person, we share the *relationship* between *u* and *X*—the connection between what about you flirts with me and the part of me needing to see that flirt.

Causal Local and Entangled Signals

Now let's examine what this relationship entanglement theory means in practice. In chapter 7, we saw that there are two types of relationship signals, those that are local and causal (you see me do "this," which causes you to do "that"), and those that are nonlocal and entangled (without even seeing me, you do "that"). Let's think first about the local, causal signals. Consider another example of you and a friend of yours. Let's imagine that you had a "bad" dream about someone hurting your feelings. As a result, you wake up in a bad mood and with your feelings hurt. If you (as *u*) are still in that victim role when you next meet your friend, she or he might respond to the local signal of your grumpy face by being nasty or parental (*X*), depending upon whether you left wanting to fight your dreamlike opponent or left in need of parental love.

In *The Dreambody in Relationships*, I said that your dream figures can "dream up" the other person's feelings, meaning that you can find someone's reactions, like your friend's nastiness or warm-heartedness, in your own dreams. "Dreaming up" means that what you experience in the outer world may be reactions to an unknown part of you seen in your dreams. In terms of the present book, it is more complete to say that your processmind seeks to express itself in a multiplicity of ways, using inner dream figures and anything and everyone in the world around you to express itself. In any case, we can speak about a "causal dreaming up" if someone responds with an *X* after seeing your *u* signals, and you can see these signals and responses in your dreams.

However, if this person's response *X* happens at a distance, without even being able to see your *u* signals, we can speak of noncausal, or entangled, nonlocal dreaming up. Thus, your feelings for the other person can be caused by a visible local signal exchange, such as smiles or grunts, or they may be entangled at a distance.

Both of these experiences—signal causality and signal entanglement—can occur at the same time. With a video camera, we can see how face-to-face interaction signals are connected in both a causal manner (your reaction follows my signal) and noncausal manner (your reaction and my signals arise at the same moment). Thus, relationships are clearly both local, meaning that *you in your body* and *me in mine* create visible reactions in one another, and, at the same time, nonlocal, meaning that our signals arise simultaneously, as if connected through the processmind.

To have a good connection with someone, follow your dreams and visible signals, and the subtle, almost invisible experience of the processmind. Remember the relationship exercise 7a from chapter 7? It had to do with the "ground of being," the processmind characteristic of relationships. From the processmind's viewpoint, we are all representatives of something larger. The processmind is just another viewpoint, but it's a key to use when nothing else works, when you find yourself in a one-sided, rigid position. Analyzing dreams and following signals are important in understanding and living together, but much more is possible when the viewpoint of the processmind is brought into relationships. The secret to relationships is the quantum theater, that is, finding the processmind, using it to flow between roles and parts, and identifying only briefly, if at all, with any one person, signal, or part.

Figure 16.4 sums up the various relationship ideas in this book. From the essence-level viewpoint, relationships are about your totem spirit, or processmind, discovering itself. This viewpoint creates a practice that is thousands of years old and still used among indigenous peoples. When Amy and I asked the African shamans how they deal with relationships (see

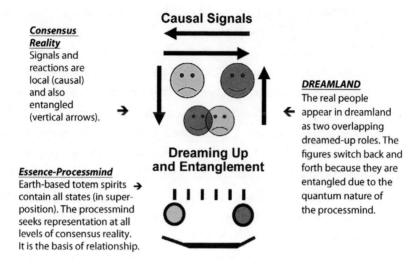

Causal Signals

Consensus Reality Signals and reactions are local (causal) and also entangled (vertical arrows).

DREAMLAND The real people appear in dreamland as two overlapping dreamed-up roles. The figures switch back and forth because they are entangled due to the quantum nature of the processmind.

Dreaming Up and Entanglement

Essence-Processmind Earth-based totem spirits contain all states (in super-position). The processmind seeks representation at all levels of consensus reality. It is the basis of relationship.

Figure 16.4. The Processmind (as a Smiling Face) in Relationship.

chapter 11), they said that they speak only briefly with the people needing help and then they send the people home. "But," I said, "how about their interchange, the face-to-face relationship connection?" The shamans said, "No, no, send them home! Don't ever tell people to talk to one another about things!" I asked, "What do you do to help?" They said something like, "Well, aha, hmm . . . we speak with the spirit." They did rituals for the spirit that connects the people in the relationship; they connected with their processminds and dealt nonlocally with the $u + X$ in relationships.

RELATIONSHIP WORK AND THE LOVE REVOLUTION

The processmind is the intelligence and power of love. I don't mean love in the sense of "being nice." I mean that love is the master facilitator process behind all relationship problems, whether personal, business, group, or international in nature. Love being, in this sense, an ineffable, essence-level phenomenon, it is beyond good and bad, nice and not so nice. It embraces the energies we like and deals well with what at first appeared to be troublesome energies.

The conscious use of the processmind in relationship is a new kind of love revolution. Whereas we like certain aspects of our friends and dislike others, the relationship processmind embraces the entire relationship and uses all its parts as phases of its overall process. In this revolution, whatever you dream or feel is both "yours" and also part of the living field of that relationship. One of the great secrets to relationships is being half in your processmind and half out. Say hello to the other person and, at the same time, open up to another level where the parts and spaceless ghosts belong as much to both of you as they do to the cosmos.

Most people wait for things to emerge from the other person in relationship. But when we are in the altered state of the processmind, we wait for identities—our own and the other person's—to submerge and then reemerge! The reality and dreaming realms work best when they are part of a process of constantly submerging and reemerging in the river of timelessness. For example, if a friend keeps forgetting to call, in consensus reality you may be angry, but at the essence level, you may already know what your friend is going to say on that call. So you can still be furious and, at the same time, not upset. In a way, at the essence level, somehow you too did not call. There is a fluid oneness, a river that zigzags along among the various parts of the situation. You are the one who is angry, you are the one who forgot to call, and you are neither—you are the flow, an omniscient, omnipresent creation that speaks for each part, one at a time, as it arises.

Is this view of relationships weird? Yes, it certainly is! But we need more than the perspective of consensus reality if we want better relationships. History shows that the human race was not born with much conscious intelligence about relationships. We need to develop our relationship intelligence, become shamans, and use altered-states awareness in the quantum theater. To help relationships, yourself, and group processes of all sorts, *be a shaman*: wait for things to emerge, but gladly submerge yourself as well, and flow back and forth between the *u* and the *X*. This approach especially helps with symmetrical accusations. In a symmetrical accusation process, each party feels that the other party caused the situation! This stance is the starting point and the fuel source for all the conflicts we experience, from everyday relationship fights to the genocides and wars.

Me: "You caused the problem."

You: "No! *You* caused the problem!"

However, if we remember the shaman's "quantum theater"—that is, the processmind that picks up and flows with or plays with all the dreaming entangled parts—then things can be bad only for a moment. We can "kill each other" with symmetrical accusations, but if we get to the processmind, that "death" can amount to detachment from our one-sided positions (at least, for a few minutes). Leave reality for a moment. Flow with the processmind and represent or "under-stand" the other's point of view. Then you may find yourself admitting, "Yes, you have an important viewpoint. From that viewpoint, *I am the problem!*" If they feel that you "under-stand" them deeply, the problem is just about solved.

A shaman goes into an altered state and shifts identities. So also, let go of your identity temporarily. Use the processmind to flow between the parts. Create a shamanistic quantum theater and act out the u and X experiences before your partner has to do it for you. As a softskill, this quantum theater will give you the most powerful relationship metaskill I know of, a skill I sometimes call the *softskill*.[1]

The following exercise can be done first as an innerwork and then, at another point, out loud as a "theater" in front of your "friend."

EXERCISE 16: THE QUANTUM ENTANGLEMENT THEATER IN RELATIONSHIPS

Choose one relationship in which symmetrical accusations or feelings sometimes occur (e.g., "Because you did *that*, I must do *this!*"). Make notes about the two viewpoints or roles that come up in that relationship during tense conflict times. Call the role you tend to play *A* and the other person's role *B*. Then remember a typical troublesome conversation where as *A* you can say and feel, "*B*, you trouble me," and as *B* you can say or feel, "If you, *A*, did not do what you do, I would not do what I do!" The idea is that neither side is admitting much of anything. The words are important, but the energy is even more important. Sketch the energies of the two roles, *A* and *B*, in square #16.

Now recall your processmind experience from chapter 15 (or the processmind of the relationship from exercise 7a in chapter 7), or locate your processmind now by recalling the deepest part of your body and its associated earth-based location. Now, while you are that location or processmind, locate the energies of *A* and *B* you just sketched as parts of your processmind's earth-based field. For example, one might be the wind, the other the trees. Or one might be the desert, the other a cactus.

Now develop the softskill. While you are still feeling that processmind, earth-based identity, stay half in and half out and create a "quantum entanglement theater." By this I mean: Be your processmind and let it experience the situation and speak it out loud to you (and/or to *B*), sensing and acting out roles as they switch back and forth between viewpoint *A* and viewpoint *B*. Let the processmind move from side to side, speaking out loud each viewpoint. As your processmind, play both roles and just notice the flow between them. As you stay close to your processmind and move from side to side, speaking for *A* and *B*, you may discover a new dimension in relationships. Then make notes about what you have discovered. Taking notes is important because of the subtle nature of some softskill experiences. In my experience, this is the most powerful personal and public conflict-resolution method available.

THE WINDY CITY QUANTUM THEATER

A woman client in my private practice used the preceding exercise to address her relationship with her husband, who, she said, constantly insulted her. To make the story short, let me briefly report on her process. Her processmind, earth-based area turned out to be a street in a large city often hit by violent winds. (See figure 16.5.) She and her partner lived in near that street, and she felt that she would have no problem becoming that amazing city street because she knew it very well and loved it. Taking the role of A, she felt like the street itself, "stable and strong." The B role in her process was her husband, who she described as nasty, puffed up, and often almost violent—like the wind. Yet he never admitted that he got into bad moods, while she had to hold their home together in spite of his temper.

After this introduction, she meditated and felt her way into her experience of the buildings, the street corner, and the wind. When she proceeded to the dialogue of her quantum entanglement theater, the following interchange emerged:

Figure 16.5. Wind over the City. A character in a client's quantum entanglement theater.

A: You hurtful man, you have insulted me! Your violent outbreaks, your addictions, make you wild and dreadful! You scare me!

B: You silly good-for-nothing! If you were not so rigid and unbending, so unfeeling and uncompromising, I would not have to blow up all the time. You drive me to drink!

A: I will not budge one single inch! I too can be nasty, really nasty!

Still in her role as *A*, she stopped and turned to me in surprise, saying that her normal behavior in the relationship was quiet and solid. "I never yell like that. When I said 'I will not budge,' I realized that I was on the other side. I felt like the wind, like my partner. I even liked that powerful wind energy!"

Smiling, she then switched roles and, as *B*, said the following:

B: I like you better this way. You are more appealing when you yell, and then I don't have to!

She was so shocked at her "theater" that she stopped at this point and smiled. Then she cried, saying, "I guess I still love him."

What happened in this inner-oriented relationship work? She experienced herself as a superposition of parts *A* and *B*. Sometimes the atmosphere around that street is quiet, sometimes it is windy, and at other times it is a combination of both. Her processmind allowed her to be a kind of shaman with the relationship softskill. She flowed back and forth between the parts of the land area: the rigid buildings on the street and the violent wind. In that way, she rediscovered not one part or the other but the flow, as well as her feelings.

Shortly thereafter, she put her newly acquired softskill to use, that is, she played all this out in front of her husband. She reported later that she enjoyed being dramatic in the quantum theater, instead of mousy as she often was in everyday life. She said the outcome was better than she had hoped. Her husband felt seen and understood by her, just as she was freed by taking on his energies. He even confessed to her that his violent energies upset him and made him afraid of himself. That is why he drank so much. He told her he had never felt so understood by her before.

Try the quantum theater with anyone with whom you want a better relationship. Develop your softskills and change the world, one relationship at a time.

THINGS TO THINK ABOUT

1. Perhaps the human race was not originally created with much relationship sense. We adults have to sometimes go back to where we came from. We need more awareness of the processmind and the way it allows us to move between entangled parts and positions.

2. If the trouble is you and me, the solution is "us," that is, the quantum theater softskill coming from the processes of our nonlocal oneness.

3. Explore this method in all kinds of personal, business, and political relationships. Practice by yourself, and bring that practice into public.

CHAPTER 17

THE WORLD AS A
CO-CREATIVE ORGANIZATION

To work with world situations, we need a global theory and associated practice. Until now, either such a theory has been missing or
the existing practices have not worked. Because processwork applies, in
principle, to organizations and groups of any kind in peaceful or chaotic
times, it could be more helpful than other organizational development
methods, which assume that groups already have an agreed-upon management method and fixed boundaries. Processwork applies to groups
of people that have no agreed-upon governing paradigm, manager, or
boundaries. It assumes instead that the governing paradigm of areas and
groups of all kinds is embedded in the processmind field of those areas
and groups.

In deep democracy, boundaries may be always changing. Why?
Because parts of any organization are nonlocal experiences. The same
is true of all consensus reality systems; they are local yet also nonlocal
and interconnected. Even the planet earth is a local/nonlocal system,
overlapping as it does with the solar system, the Milky Way (our gal-
axy system), and the entire universe. The simplest consensual definition
of an organization is a group of people working toward shared goals.
If we add to this a more deeply democratic organizational view that
includes different awareness levels, we have a model that looks like the
facilitator's processmind as illustrated in figure 8.1 in chapter 8. If we

add entanglement to that model, we arrive at a model of the world as an entangled, co-creative organization (see figure 17.1). This approach creates an innerwork practice and dynamic group method of working with teams, groups, and world situations.

Knowledge and experience of an organization's processmind allow it to function more easily and successfully. Without attention paid to the processmind, organizations lack cohesiveness and fall asunder because the members become unconscious of the inspiration they all potentially share. Then people freeze into their consensus reality roles and become "squares." Bringing the processmind's entanglement into full relief as a living theater enables groups of all kinds to discover and develop their own internal self-organizing ability to fulfill and sustain their missions by flowing between dreamland roles.

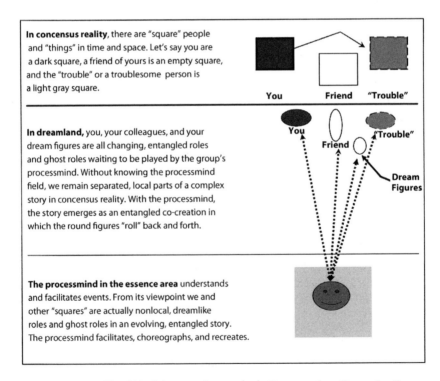

Figure 17.1. The World as an Entangled, Co-creative Organization.

Organizations can be managed from the bottom up, following the "body" and (socially) low-ranking people, or from the top down, following the "head" and the high-ranking people. Both methods can be important at one time or another, but neither is sustainable. Following only the body (without the head) may create a needed revolution. Following solely the head creates autocracies or oligarchies (leadership by the few). Yet a democracy is based upon power no less than an autocracy is: the majority rules. This is an improvement over a dictatorship, but without recognition of the deeper democracy and the processmind, too much power still remains in everyone's head!

A PLANETARY PERSPECTIVE

From the viewpoint of deep democracy, the world itself is an organization with at least one shared goal among its multitudinous parts: most people want to survive. The major question we all need to answer is: how do we survive best, not just moment to moment, but in a sustainable way? Obviously, we need to reduce war and preserve our biosphere. During the past few hundred years, individuals and major world powers alike have been oriented toward themselves and have neglected until recently the increase of earth-based issues, such as our troubled biosphere, global warming, and unsustainable use of natural resources. In chapter 10, I spoke about using the earth to contact the processmind for group processes connected with catastrophes such as Hurricane Katrina in New Orleans.

To work on any global problem, we need a planetary viewpoint. The motto "Think globally, act locally" has been important since the late 1960s. The "brown politics" suggested in this book involve a relationship paradigm that says, for example, "Be a real person, and also be the earth to choreograph her parts as they tangle-dance," that is, as they interact in the quantum theater. Whatever we do without this "dance" yields unsustainable results, or even unnecessary conflict and failure. To save ourselves and the biosphere, we need to *be* the whole earth's processmind while working *with* the earth's parts.

We need quantum theater's systemic, nonlocal approach to move beyond solving one problem or another in a causal manner. Solving problems in a fix-it mood is obviously important. Save energy! Save water! But without reference to the entire system, to the planet, fixing one problem will simply cause another and not necessarily create more community.

Is the system that of the planet Gaia? Well, yes, in the first approximation. But Gaia is mainly associated with homeostatic environmental processes that supposedly create environments hospitable for biological life. We need to expand beyond our focus on biological life to a new life concept, one that is more "mythostatic," that is, one that focuses upon the planet earth and its ecological communities and, at the same time, upon the deepest sense and meaning of life.

In the view of brown politics, cultural experience of the earth's nature in a given location is the power behind that culture's vision and direction. The earth is the creator of cultural myths. She is real, and she is also the power giving rise to creation in the physical and mythic sense. At different times, the human race may even fear death or extinction, not only because of the real problems facing us, but because we "need" to drop our individual human identities to rediscover and co-create our future. We need to be the spirit of the Big Bang, Genesis, Unkulunkulu, Pachamama, or creation or whatever we may call that processmind. Just as each individual in a relationship has her or his own experience of that relationship's processmind, so each individual, group, and culture has its own experience of the earth's basic nature. Getting in touch with that processmind's nature will help manage all kinds of global problems, including ethnic conflicts, environmental trouble, and war. The earth's processmind could help us relate better and swing in a quantum theater, tangle-dancing between the various polarities and roles, however each of us defines them.

Consider the physical earth; she is a five-billion-year-old planet. In figure 17.2, you can see some of her various physical levels. On her surface, she is home to millions of living species. Yet her crust upon which

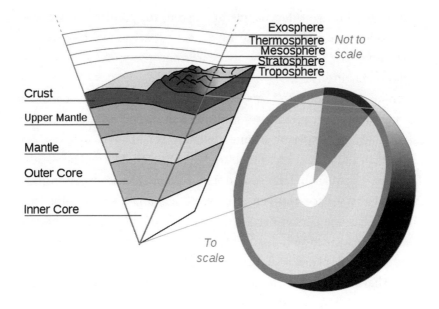

Figure 17.2. The Planet Earth and Her Core.

we live is only a very thin skin. Beneath are many chemically active layers. She has an inner core that in size is about 70 percent of the size of the moon and may be hotter than the sun's surface. She interacts with other planets and outer space, all the while revolving around the sun together with other parts of our solar system.

At the same time, our earth is a multidimensional, dreamlike goddess that has been imaged, for example, as the Pachamama of the Incas, a goddess who creates earthquakes as well as fertility for human crops. She is also an unnamable essence that some of us consciously feel, breathe into, relate to, and become.

ELDERSHIP

This real and also dreamlike planet is the major part of everyone's growing planetary eldership. This eldership is created via our ability to connect not only to other people but also to the earth's own wisdom. This wisdom can guide us in caring for her surface as we all move with her through the universe. The real earth and the moon inspire us to dream (see figure 17.3).

In my 1980s book *The Year One*, I wrote that we need one person in one hundred in any given community to pull that community together. But finding that one person is quite a job. That person needs to have access to the earth and to her or his processmind, to hear all sides and be all sides, and to be a shaman and tangle-dance in a quantum theater that includes events at the surface and beneath, events in human communities and dreams. That one person needs a second training. Recall that while the first training focuses on skills, the second focuses on access to the process-mind and to this planet in all her forms. Whereas the first training focuses upon what we might call "hard skills," such as facilitating signal exchange in communications, the second training gives us the "soft skills" or emotional intelligence needed to get along with others and the universe.

Developing this second training leadership is important. I don't believe we need more powerful leaders. What this planet needs are team creators: individuals with a softskill (e.g., access to the processmind) who

Figure 17.3. Earth and Full Moon.

can help all of us work together by relating more deeply to one another and to all parts of the system. Imagine co-creating teams not just from your circle of friends but with individuals, groups, and nations that don't like either you or each other! That's our next big job: creating teamwork that includes animals, plants, rocks, people, machines, and especially people we don't like! We need facilitators who understand process-oriented ecology and who can recycle our physical and psychological trash: reuse both cardboard and psychological projections, reuse plastic and also ghost roles to unclog our "rivers." We need people who are as attached to the earth's core as they are to people, animals, and plants—people who can work with relationships at all levels.

How do we develop the needed skills in ourselves? The moment-to-moment answer is "Dislike the trouble, note its energy, drop into the earth, and flow with the troublesome energy!" Every time you see junk, *use it*. Recycle it. Be it, then be the one who cleans it all up. Whenever you meet an oppressor, bring that figure onto the stage in the quantum theater, both alone and with others. Become all the various parts right away! Do the tangle-dance! Entanglement will help that person step out of the oppressor's role and enable everyone to use that energy in a way that better serves the whole.

THE PROCESSMIND IN ACTION

Can one person in a hundred, or even a thousand, make a difference? Yes! How do I know? I have seen such tangle-dances happen. In my *Sitting in the Fire*, I wrote about one of the most memorable events of my life. I must recall that event again here because it shows how the one person who is needed may spontaneously appear during troubled times. It occurred in 1992 at a tense open forum and large group process that Amy and I were facilitating in Oakland, California, just days before the verdict of the Rodney King trial. We were there together with other colleagues and friends in part because of the severe racial tension in the air.

The problem began in 1991, when Los Angeles police were videotaped beating an African American taxi driver, Rodney King, who had been speeding. The police were brought to trial, and, despite very damning evidence, the jury acquitted them. Immediately after that trial, racial tension erupted in many U.S. cities, and in Los Angeles itself the rioters numbered in the thousands. By the time the police, the U.S. Army, and the Marines restored order, the casualties included 55 deaths, 2,383 injuries, more than 7,000 fires, damages to 3,100 businesses, and nearly $1 billion in financial losses.

We were working with hundreds of people on the theme of racism just days before those riots, and the situation in the meeting hall was extremely tense. Imagine hundreds of people, full of pain and anger, hoping to right the wrongs that had been done. Imagine them yelling, screaming at one another . . . all at the same time.

In the midst of that painful situation, one man stepped forward and began moaning quietly to himself. At first, few saw or heard him. Slowly he moved forward from the outskirts of that large group into the midst of the violent discussion, all the while sinking more deeply into himself. He came to the middle of the room where everyone was standing around in a circle. His moan increased until it became a cry as he began to sway on his feet, first to one side, then the other. He moaned and then cried out in the rhythm of his body movements, "This is not black pain, it is not white pain, this is all our pain." This black man began to cry, he wailed as he "sang," swaying first on one foot then on the other. The atmosphere was intense. At first a couple of people went over to him to hold him. Soon everyone in that meeting hall began encircling that one man who had spontaneously contacted his processmind, which embraced all the parts in conflict. He was moaning and wailing, half-speaking, half-singing, while swaying in such a way that everyone, black people, white people, were all moved to tears.

The whole group came together, huddling around him, around his passion and pain for one side and then the other side. In his own way, he embraced, felt, and then spoke for everyone in a kind of quantum theater. Soon one person, then another, began to speak. Others fell silent and listened. After individuals spoke, groups representing different ages, races, and regions spontaneously and proudly came forward, one after the other, to sing the songs that expressed the numinousness of their cultures. The feeling in that room was, and still is, indescribable. After about a half an hour, everyone began to work organically together on the painful issues at hand, as if directed by some unseen force.

UNITIVE CONSCIOUSNESS

That one gifted man had access to the unitive consciousness of his processmind. Everyone could feel it. When he wailed, sang, and spoke, every single person in the room was touched. Just as important as the resulting vibrant atmosphere was the passionate enthusiasm people felt to communicate about themselves and work together. And equally important to these results in the moment was a result that could not be seen until later. When riots broke out in cities across the United States in response to the trial verdict a few days later, the San Francisco–Oakland area was one of the only metropolitan regions with a large African American population that did *not* erupt in destructive riots and open conflict. The *San Francisco Chronicle* credited that fact to what had happened in our meeting.[1] Perhaps group and city ecological process are closely linked or entangled for worse, or, in this case, for better.

The newspaper praised Amy and me. But we were less important than that single man. With his own spontaneous, processmind experience, he was more advanced in group work than we were at the time. If one person can have such a huge impact on such a large and intense conflict, turning it into conscious co-creation through relationship to his deepest self, imagine what a few such people could do for the whole planet. I am reminded of the Rev. Howard Thurman, a student of Gandhi and apparently one of Martin Luther King, Jr.'s mentors and spiritual teachers. In 1944, Thurman founded one of the first racially integrated, multicultural churches in the United States. In his essay "The Search For Common Ground: An Inquiry into the Basis of Man's Experience of Community," he writes:

> In the conflicts between man and man, between group and group, between nation and nation, the loneliness of the seeker for community is sometimes unendurable. The radical tension between good and evil, as man sees it and feels it, does not have the last word about the meaning of life and the nature of existence. . . . Always he must know that the contradictions of life are not final or ultimate; he must distinguish between failure and a many-sided awareness. . . . He will . . . perceive harmony that transcends all diversities and in which diversity finds its richness and significance.[2]

Dr. Thurman advises against dealing only with the immediate surface problems. He goes on to say, "Don't ask yourself what the world needs. Ask yourself what makes you come alive and then go do that. Because what the world needs is people who have come alive."[3]

EXERCISE 17: THE FACILITATOR'S POWER DANCE FOR ORGANIZATIONS

To help yourself and the world, we need to know, dear reader, what makes you come alive. In terms of the present book, the deepest answer is your processmind or the processmind of a city or bioregion and the manner in which it brings entangled parts and their interactions fluidly to life. The following innerwork preparation for large group (and organizational) work is based upon "what makes you come alive," namely, the earth-based totem spirit of the area. Find that power that makes you come alive and live it by feeling its nonlocal omnipresence while acting locally in the public domain. You can use this exercise with any organization, including your own family, which is, by the way, perhaps one of the most difficult of all world groups.

Following the group's processmind will enable you to "sing" and move in a way that catalyzes others to "sing" as well, to tangle-dance, so to speak. This processmind will connect to, and flow with, playing all the group roles as if they were yours, because in a nonlocal sense, they are your own. Practice this exercise with friends (or, to begin with, imagine two friends playing out typical organizational or family roles for you). We shall be seeking the processmind's rhythm and movement "power dance." The movements and the experience will inform you about what to do and how to create a theater. This processmind and power dance are your potential "gifts" to the world.

To begin, choose the most difficult family, business, group, organizational, or world problem you can think of. Who or what people/roles are involved? Which is the most troublesome; that is, which role or person or group upsets you the most? Call that role *B*. What role do you typically play? Call that *A*. Now imagine and feel *A* and *B* briefly and make a hand gesture that goes with each side of the issue. Make a note about or sketch *A* and *B*'s energies in the corner of your collage square #17.

Now what is the family, business, or group's typical room and/or atmosphere? This can be a wonderful or terrible atmosphere. The important thing is to find a typical one! Stand and sense that room or atmosphere, feel it all around you. While feeling it, breathe into that atmosphere. Is it violent, heavy, tense, depressed, lofty, or beautiful? Make a face to show that atmosphere. Feel the atmosphere again, make that face, and let the atmosphere move you a little. And while you are moving and breathing into this atmosphere, associate this experience with an earth-based, natural area. Go there and feel yourself at that spot. Sense the power and force of that spot and notice how it affects your body. Take your time with that altered state. When you get a good sense of it, feel how the power of that spot begins to move you into a dance. Let it dance you until you feel that *you are that spot moving you, you are that force and earth energy with its power dance.* As you dance, sense the message your dance is expressing.

Then let that earth spot and dance make a quick sketch of itself on the collage pages in square #17. Make notes about what the spot/dance said about itself. In what way does this dance make you "come alive"? Make a note about that. Now feel and do that processmind power dance again and as you do it, speak to your everyday self as *A* about this dance experience. And still in that dance when you are ready, remember *B*, the troublesome situation, person, or people, and notice how the processmind power dance deals with the situation in its own way, with its dance and altered state. Now as your processmind, make sounds and motions and practice playing and even dancing roles *A* and *B*. Give each time and focus. How are both of these roles part of you as the processmind? Imagine doing this with the real people in that organization. Your body will tell you when you are done.

Working with the Kitchen Table

The following example of this exercise is extracted from a verbatim report. I have made changes only to protect the identities of those involved.

Louise: I have not lived at home for many years, so I returned back to my family to get to know them again. It is the hardest thing I have ever done. . . . In my family there is something so dead . . . so ugly and muted, almost suffocating. . . . In the background is the Holocaust and great loss. So there is violence, death; only one person of my family lived through it, and that was my father. Concentration camps, gas chambers, ghettos—it's heavy. Now my father's mind is going a bit

. . . and he talks about that awful historical piece of his life a lot, even though he never talked about it before.

The role that troubles me in that family scene is the one his partner plays. She gets fed up with him as he becomes more magical, more different, and she cannot stand it. About dementia, she said, "You really do think about euthanasia." When she said that I thought, oh my god, as he ages must he face the same force that had already threatened to kill him before—that is, if you are not normal, you must die?

The roles and energies in that family scene are all me, both the one trying to bring awareness to the situation and my stepmother's murderous or cold nature. Brrrr! The typical room or atmosphere of the family is the kitchen. I hate that kitchen! It is really just . . . stark . . . and flimsy . . . the kitchen has this terrible table that everyone sits around. That table is wobbly! If you move in a certain way, something is going to flop down. And the chairs are really uncomfortable, and everything they do to that kitchen to improve it is just more awful!

After meditating upon the atmosphere of that kitchen, Louise went on with the exercise.

LOUISE: The essence of that kitchen table area and atmosphere . . . hmmm . . . reminds me for some reason of a very mountainous part of Tasmania, the island off the coast of Australia. It is full of this sharp grass . . . if your leg brushes against it, you end up with scratches. But the mountains are incredible. It is cold and yet a beautiful place . . . gorgeous . . . when I go there . . . oh, I had a sudden flash of insight coming from the land. Tasmania said, "Where are my people?" I think of the genocide there of the indigenous people—they were completely wiped out . . . [cries, big breaths].

Louise then enters into the quantum theater created and facilitated by her processmind and plays out the roles and process between herself and her stepmother.

LOUISE AS STEP-MOTHER: As the partner, I must "scratch," I must say that I too suffer. . . . I saw this incredible TV program about euthanasia, killing people to put them out of their misery.

LOUISE AS HERSELF: [listens and then reacts] I must put my hand in front of you, Stepmother! I don't want you to say those things! No! Not another Holocaust. [Then cooler and more detached from her processmind experience] Stepmother, I want to give you some help. I think you need somebody to talk to. I think you are so lonely in this whole experience, I think, wow, how hard it must be that you had that thought . . . how awful and how you must suffer. Oh! How heartbreaking . . . how awful to think that about your husband. It is really heartbreaking to . . . watch that TV show and think that at the end of it . . . death would come as a relief. I feel so sad for you.

LOUISE AS STEP-MOTHER: I feel like I am going to cry now . . . I won't . . . yes, I will . . . God, I really could cry.

Louise stepped out of the entangled process and said, "I never realized how incredibly alone my stepmother is. What an insight."

That was the end of Louise's family quantum theater with us. It helped her return home and complete her tangle-dance process there. She let us know that once back at that kitchen table, she and her stepmother "danced," that is, they had the first of a number of more intimate and supportive interactions, unlike any they had ever had in the thirty-five years of their relationship. She also let us know that a month or so later, her stepmother replaced that awful kitchen table and bought a new sturdy one that the whole family can sit around comfortably.

YOUR GIFT

What can we learn from such experiences that connect environmental situations, historical difficulties, trauma, and renewal of relationships? Again, Howard Thurman suggests: "Don't ask yourself what the world needs. Ask yourself what makes you come alive and then give that. Because what the world needs is people who have come alive." Don't focus only on the solutions to problems; focus on the earth spirit that "brings you alive." What brings you to life is potentially your greatest gift to the world.

Our earth knows how to handle her problems.[4] Even the most terrible atmosphere, even an old, dingy kitchen table and its atmosphere, has a sacred piece of nature associated with it. The presence of the earth "knows" how to transform every "kitchen table." The most dreadful family atmosphere, the tensest organization, the bloodiest war or worst ecological world region may seem hopeless until we engage in the earth's tangle-dance, which knows how to move beyond both good and bad. Instead of ignoring or fighting the world's problems, whether the smallest or the most global, go deeper to "under-stand" them as the beginning of a new story.

Being our local selves while also engaging in the nonlocal tangle-dance with all the aspects of the situation brings hope, even where there was little beforehand. Follow Pachamama as she reorganizes our planet so we can all sit around the table together. To begin with, like the man in Oakland, you may feel alone in the midst of hundreds. But you are not alone when you follow your processmind, for you touch and remind the rest of us that, by following the earth, we re-create the community we have always wanted.

THINGS TO THINK ABOUT

Even the worst team, group, or ecological atmosphere is associated with an important place on earth. To help the earth, be the planet and tangle-dance her parts.

CONCLUSION

UBUNTU,
THE WORLD'S FUTURE

The best conclusion to a book is probably the reader's own reflections on what he or she has experienced while reading. (For this reason, I have included three additional squares labeled "Loveland" at the end of the collage pages.) Along with most people, you probably identify yourself in everyday reality as a particular person, a body changing in time. But from the viewpoint of the processmind, you are a field with both local and nonlocal connections, an altered state of consciousness associated with the deepest feeling in your body, and a favorite place on earth. I often call that place "Loveland." Loveland is where you come from; it is your dreammaker, the core of your ability to interconnect and tangle with everyone and everything.

Take some time to browse through your experiences as recorded on the collage pages in appendix B. Notice what earth-based locations occurred frequently in association with your processmind experiences. Make a note about the nature of these places on the collage pages in the square called "Loveland, Your Home Area." Again look through the sketches and ideas on your collage pages and notice any common processmind elements that seem central. Then fill in the last two boxes, sketching in the "Loveland Energy Sketch" box a common energy form you see in your collage of drawings and writing in the "Loveland Content Summary" a sentence about the common ideas you notice. Please take the time to note and reflect on your answers.

Consider the possibility of "wearing your nature," by which I mean *being* it as you move through the world. "Wearing your nature" reminds me of a photograph of a Huli wigman of Papua New Guinea (see figure C.1). This self-decoration seems to me symbolic of "wearing" the processmind.

Until now, I have tried to show that the processmind is central to psychology and spiritual traditions and basic to deep democracy in politics. The processmind is a psychological pattern analogous to the quantum-wave function in physics that structures entanglement and time reversibility. The processmind is usually an invisible field that

Figure C.1. A Huli Wigman of
Papua, New Guinea.

tends to move our bodies and organize our dreams, environments, and nations. In many ways, our sentient body experience is like a compass needle or pendulum, moved by an invisible field. We can sometimes say no to that field, for we have the ability to move as we like—at least for short periods. Yet, when we are exhausted, we are forced to sense once again the uncanny tendency to turn in this direction or that without knowing exactly what the field is. Unless we do some form of meditation to get in touch with that field, we may have only flickering insights of the processmind as the origin of awareness and consciousness. Nevertheless, we must conclude, it is a self-organizing, self-reflecting mysterious space between us and all things. I have pointed out in this book how Aboriginal peoples honor this field's strength in terms of what they variously call "power spots," "totem spirits," and the "Dreaming."

Processmind pulls together "mind of God" speculations in physics with the structure of God experiences in spiritual traditions. The processmind is an attempt to find common ground in process-oriented psychology and other psychological schools seeking to understand the guiding intelligence seen, for example, behind our dreams. The processmind brings psychology closer to the earth and our politics closer to gravity. Just as we feel drawn toward the earth because of a mixture of gravity and psychology, just as we are drawn to certain places on earth, the earth, too, is drawn toward the sun. Together with other planets, our earth creates the solar system. Likewise, our system connects with the Milky Way and the rest of the universe. The practical message of all this is that, like it or not, we are in a community with all things. We are at least in community with the rest of our world, our planet . . . and perhaps the whole universe.

In an attempt to expand psychology to apply to all human activity and to relate more completely to the universe, I stepped out farther into noncognitive regions of experience than some readers may be familiar with. In earlier chapters, I focused mostly on our psychology, showing how processmind field theory organizes not only flickering, flirt-like body experiences, but relationships, small teams, and city and world events. I am thankful that the processmind idea found a related concept in Zen's "empty mind." Remember Suzuki's Zen mind analogy. On dark nights, like the empty mind, the invisible electric field between heaven and earth precedes the blasts of lightning that amaze our senses.

The lightning streaks are so awesome that we are in danger of forgetting the field that preceded and will persist after them. Likewise, what happens in life seems impressive, so good or so bad that we often overlook the incredibly subtle processmind field in the background. The events we see are important, but so is the field behind those events. Suzuki equated knowledge of that field with enlightenment.

The understanding that the processmind field is always present in and around you leads to a useful practice you can do anywhere: tracking your body tendencies and seeking the message that lies behind them. Remember the deepest part of yourself in your body and its associated "Loveland" location, which holds the palpable experience connecting parts and people that you may have thought were separated. Loveland facilitates interactions and understands parts, not as rigid states but as phases of itself. It appears as the atmosphere around the part of your own living space you love the most. Look around where you are right now. Find the spot you like the best. The experiences you get there show that your guide is always near you.

Access to the processmind's Loveland can reduce fear of what the future might bring. It allows you a kind of stillness in the midst of dynamic movement, as if you are the weight itself at the bottom of a swinging pendulum (see figure C.2). You are grounded, yet you can feel and swing with the earth's wavy field lines, with the things that move you right and left, both in the diverse "sides" of yourself and the world around you. This experience is different from the typically rigid stance we take toward change, a stance that does not swing and therefore makes us fear that we will be overtaken or broken.

When you lose track of that field (or when it marginalizes itself), the pains of life hurt much more! Body symptoms, for instance, appear as foreign and unwanted phenomena. But with awareness of the process-

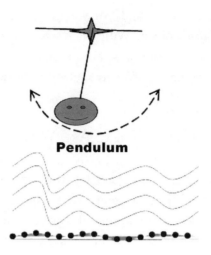

Figure C.2. Loveland Earth.

mind field, those symptoms' energies become reminders of your internal diversity, your entire self. There is nothing wrong with treating your local body as a machine that sometimes needs fixing. But the body that is hearing or looking at these words just now is not just a machine. And you are not its only boss. In fact, the body that you feel is "yours" is an incomplete picture of you. It is not your whole experience. Don't forget your processmind's subtle, nonlocal presence. While refreshing your face each morning, refresh your body image as well by remembering the earth from which you came. As you dress, also put on your earth-based "clothes," that is, the trees and mountains, the landscape, and the city street corner that you are.

The consensus-reality view of relationships hypnotizes us into thinking they are composed of two or more people and/or things. But that is not the whole truth. Without awareness of the unifying space that surrounds and pervades the relationship, the two or more of us are literally up in the air—that is, not "grounded" in what "under-stands" us. If conflict arises in a relationship, then begin with what you notice: Be one-sided. Start to fight. But then remember to "die" before "war" breaks out, thereby bringing the entanglement dance to life. The roles saying,

"You made me act this way!" and "No, you made me do what I did!" are then inside and outside of you. With awareness of your deepest self, you can then shift from being only a part of the action to being also the storymaker, the choreographer, of an entangled co-creation.

GOD, WHERE ARE YOU?

In rereading this book, I was again touched by Mother Teresa's cry, "O God, are you there?" Her plea reminded me of Einstein, Schrödinger, and other scientists who felt that their discoveries had not yet led them nearer to any grasp of divine force or intelligence. We saw in chapter 1 Einstein's lament: "Quantum mechanics is certainly imposing. But an inner voice tells me that it is not yet the real thing. The theory says a lot, but does not really bring us any closer to the secret of the Old One."[1]

Mother Teresa's misgivings and Einstein's doubting "inner voice" were looking for the "real thing." Their doubting minds sensed that the "Old One" must be present. But where? I hope to have shown in this book that our seeking of that Old One, the "mind of God," is the mind of God seeking itself. Physics almost knows this from its theories! Physicists speak about self-reflecting wave functions in space and about the nonlocality of particles. They just do not yet realize—or some may even resist the idea—that these functions refer not only to mathematical but also to psychological hyperspaces.

At present, science and religion generally agree upon one thing: they disagree. Religion speaks about the structure of hyperspaces in terms of omniscience, omnipotence, omnipresence, and flow, whereas science refers to math and nonlocality. From the processmind point of view, the conflict between religion and science is in fact needed. By doubting each other, everyone collaborates in the ongoing story I call "entangled co-creation." While this process of co-creation itself is a constant, the stories it creates about the nature of our universe will always—I guess—be changing.

Nonlocality in physics and psychology points to the reason why innerwork is outer work as well. All our innerwork is world work, and world work is our innerwork. Your psychology is not contained by your physical boundary; you can't have a personal psychology that belongs only to you. This means that in the altered state of consciousness characteristic of the dreaming process, parts of the universe become your family and your community. What you experience is a piece of the universe *experiencing you*. The world in which we live is a community made of nonlocal energies and life forms emerging into separable yet entangled bi-localities and the consensus reality of everyday life.

Diagrams stressing unified field theories to clarify this community idea are important, but I have placed my own speculations about unified field theories at the end of appendix A. Why? Because evolving theory is important, but it is not the main point of this book. Theory does not tell us *how* to live in a moment-to-moment manner in the midst of the turmoil of everyday life. Theory helps us answer Einstein's questing: "I want to know God's thoughts . . . all the rest are details." But I would like to say to Einstein: Theories do not tell us how to make a better world. The "details," dear Dr. Einstein, are the ways to practice what we know.

Einstein's brilliant discovery of the energy-mass equivalence, namely $E = mc^2$, helped us understand atomic energy, but the hard skills of that theory—how to generate nuclear energy—were not enough to stop us from dropping atomic bombs. A theory in science (like an idea in psychology or a belief in religion) is *never* complete without the details, that is, how to use it to make life better for everyone. We need all the hard cognitive knowledge and associated cognitive hard skills and intelligence we can get. But cognitive skills are not enough to resolve human problems. We also need to awaken. We need the feeling wisdom, the softskills, to deal with the complexities of everyday life.

The most useful human softskill for our times is one that ensures the best possible future for this planet. Given the conflictual nature of the problems the world faces today, this skill would prioritize the capacity to experience all sides as important, even as phases of one another. The processmind practice is such a softskill. Applying this softskill makes every personal, relational, and world conflict a doorway to the infinite. But I would never be satisfied with this theory if it did not show you, in your personal innerwork and outer mediation practices, how to transform fighters into dancers. If this theory as presented in this book has not yet taught you how to do this, please—for me and everyone else—update the ideas herein so that they work better!

UBUNTU AND WORLD FUTURES

I have always been touched by the concept of *ubuntu*, the powerful community ethic of Central and South Africa. In Zulu, *ubuntu* means: "The belief in a universal bond of sharing that connects all humanity."[2] Nelson Mandela, anti-apartheid activist and former president of South Africa, describes the ubuntu ethic concisely: "I am because you are."[3] This ethic, which is basic to South Africa's "truth and reconciliation" policies, epitomizes the essence of entanglement and community thinking: "If it were not for you, I would not be here, and if you were not here, I would not be here either." (See figure C.3 for a visual expression of this ethic.)

From the processmind point of view, ubuntu is based upon quantum entanglement, the nonlocal, dreamlike link between everyone and everything in a diverse community—in fact, the whole universe. In other words, we are in relationship with everything that "flirts" with us: "I am because you are." Our human community is because of all the other human and nonhuman communities in the universe. Ubuntu is a kind of process oriented ecology, in the sense that one part of an ecosystem comes to life through its local and nonlocal connection with all the other parts.

It seems to me that ubuntu is associated with other important community ideas, such as *ahimsa*, or nonviolence, brought to world prominence by Gandhi. This concept, which is common to Hinduism, Buddhism, and Jainism, is the preeminent practice of Jainism.[4] In the Jain symbol (pictured in figure C.4), the wheel, the *dharma chakra*, symbol-

Figure C.3. *Ubuntu*, a Batik by Richard Kimbo.

izes the 360-degree, all-around commitment to stop harm and repetitive conflicts, that is, the cycle of reincarnation through nonviolence. The script in the middle of the wheel reads "ahimsa." Awareness of the processmind, which is a key concept in this book, aligns with and supports ahimsa, in that it prevents us from being one-sided and only our consensus reality selves.

Ubuntu and ahimsa are important concepts. Their sources must have been earth-based experience. Within the processmind's living quantum theater, such symmetrical statements as "I am because you are" become dynamic relationship processes in which "I" and "you" are no longer distant or even in separate localities. We are one locality in two places, so to speak. Informed by processmind experience, we know distance and also intimate closeness with all beings. The processmind softskill enables even your worst enemy to feel "under-stood by you." If you stay "half in

Figure C.4. The Jain Symbol for Ahimsa.

Loveland, half out" while working with severe disagreements, you can feel yourself swing from one side to the other as what was "you" becomes something like "the other." The processmind softskill then becomes a kind of song and feeling, like singing while you work, dancing while facilitating the resolution to world problems.

This reminds me of the U.S. civil rights marches in the 1960s, when the African American community co-created a new world in the United States. They sang, for example, "We Shall Overcome" while peacefully interacting with backlash from mainstream America. I clearly remember people singing the chorus of that song:[5]

Oh deep in my heart
I do believe
We shall overcome some day.

Overcome what? One-sidedness, separation, and repression—at least for a moment, if not longer. My point is that "deep in everyone's heart" is a tangle-dance that facilitates and draws together apparently separate, conflicting parts so that each voice feels needed for the whole song. If you listen closely, you can almost hear the processmind assuring those who sing that although they may feel alone, they are not. In fact, they are nonlocally connected.

> We are not alone
> We are not alone
> We are not alone today
>
> *Chorus:*
> The whole wide world around
> The whole wide world around
> The whole wide world around some day. . . .

At the end of chapter 17, I said that when you begin the quantum entanglement "dance," flowing between positions, at first conflicting parties will look at your tangle-dance as if they are an audience that is either for or against what is happening. But eventually, that tangle-dance touches others. Many will want to join, being reminded of their deepest selves, as we saw in the story of the man who "danced" in Oakland, pulling hundreds of us together.

Such stories are worth remembering, because the daily news can make us feel hopeless about the state of the world. Recall the big picture: Our human race is still young, only about two hundred thousand years old. In comparison, our earth is about five billion years old. In a way, we are tiny babies born just yesterday. So it's okay to be critical, but it's also important to be patient with ourselves.

Individual and community ethics are always changing, and each century seems to need a new multicultural ethics. Today we need an ethics that honors history and also reaches into the future, drawing on methods found in the oldest spiritual traditions and the newest cutting-edge sciences. We need an ethics that includes but goes beyond "doing good." The process I call "entangled co-creation" is such a new ethics. In small and very large groups, it can turn an apparent clash of civilizations into a community experience where just about everyone feels heard and at home.

When you dance in that entanglement theater, you feel new changes unfolding that you did not believe could ever happen. At first the change may be the appearance of a tiny smile brightening the face of an "opponent." Something touched her or him. Then, in spite of yourself, your face, too, may begin to glow a little. These brighter faces are the change that is needed. They are the flash of lightning from the dark night's sky. These are the faces that lead us into the future. When you see them, you can understand why I call this book *Processmind: A User's Guide to Connecting with the Mind of God*.

Appendix A

Quantum Mind Update

The processmind appears in the quantum world in terms of what I call the "quantum mind." In my book *The Quantum Mind and Healing*, I focus upon psychological processes projected onto or discovered in quantum physics. In brief, my idea of the quantum mind comes from the structures I see in the math of quantum physics. I call the conjugation of the wave function that is needed to create an observation "self-reflection." Physics itself offers no explanation for conjugation. In *Quantum Mind*, I suggest that conjugation and reflection arise from the quantum-mind aspects of nature, from an innate "curiosity" of the universe to know itself. The quantum mind is the tendency of both material nature and our psychology to:

1. **Self-reflect**, or conjugate the wave function to create "reality" through "flirts."
2. **Superpose**, that is, to sum up all vectors and histories (as in the math of quantum physics). In psychology, this sum appears as the sum of our directions. The resulting direction is our basic nature, our myth, a direction I call the "big U." The quantum mind organizes that sum of directions over time to zigzag freely, constrained only by the overall direction or personal myth. (See my *Earth-Based Psychology* for more on this topic.)

3. **Guide us**. David Bohm suggested that the quantum wave is a "pilot wave" (or quantum potential) that guides particles through their trajectories. The sense of "guidance" is basic to psychology. In *Quantum Mind*, I suggest that the quantum mind's piloting function is often experienced as an accidental or unintentional "field" that moves us. With awareness, the quantum mind becomes an "intentional field" or "force of silence." This force moves you silently through the night and through the "darkness" of the day. In this present book, this quantum potential or intentional field appears as what Aboriginal people have always sensed as an earth-based power, a psychophysical body experience I call the "processmind."

4. **Marginalize** parts and states and create reality by "collapsing" itself (in the mathematical form of the wave function.) Physics implies that the collapse reduces all the possibilities to basically one result; for example, Schrödinger's cat is no longer both dead and alive, as it was before observation. Rather, after observation it "collapses" to one or the other. In psychology, however, there is no true collapse. We are in the here and now of "reality," while other possibilities are still in the background as dreamlike flirts and double signals. We can marginalize dreaming to feel more real, but the truth is, we can be both in one place at one time and simultaneously in other places and times. There is no true collapse; there is just a marginalization of dreaming. My guess is that the rest of nature is the same. There is no collapse; there is just a marginalization.

5. **Entangle parts nonlocally**, as we have seen in this book.

In my *Quantum Mind and Healing* and especially in *Earth-Based Psychology*, the quantum mind was characterized mainly by its quantum world characteristics. In this book, I am proposing that the processmind contains all of the quantum mind's self-reflecting, superposing, marginalizing, and entanglement characteristics but also moves beyond agreed-upon concepts of quantum physics. For the individual human being, the quantum mind is a force field experience, a palpable, nonlocal, earth-based field that appears in what Aboriginal peoples call "totem spirits." The processmind emerges as a fieldlike presence we can feel at every moment, including in the form of spontaneous flirts. The processmind is the organizer of our awareness and consciousness.

As far as I know at present, the processmind force field can be felt, but its experience has not been measured. In physics, the processmind appears in Bohm's idea of the "pilot wave," in Aboriginal experience as totem spirits, and in organizational work and politics as system minds. At the essence level, the processmind is like the Tao that can't be said. When it can be said, that is, at the dreamland and consensus reality levels, it appears as dream symbols or basic concepts such as the Self in psychology, quantum waves in physics, and the gods in spiritual traditions and politics. Perhaps the processmind is or will contribute to a "unified field theory." I discussed in chapter 14 of this book how the four force fields of physics—electromagnetism, the strong and weak forces, and gravity—may eventually be combined by some TOE (theory of everything). In terms of physics, a unified field theory is one possible TOE.

While such theories of everything are problematic because they are speculative, thinking about them is important because they point to the sense we have of an underlying pattern, or "mind of God," and that pattern needs to be reformulated and updated again and again over time to fit the language and times of a given people. Nevertheless, it is unlikely that any one verbal or mathematical formula will be able to express the entirety of the processmind's sentient essence and power, which seems to lie at the limits of our cognitive comprehension.

Psychology, physics, spiritual traditions, and community all have their own TOEs, which are more or less separate from each other. Figuratively speaking, if we add the processmind to these TOEs, a "foot" emerges. The processmind is both a "foot," pulling the various TOEs together, and at the same time the name for the big TOE, as represented in figure A.1.

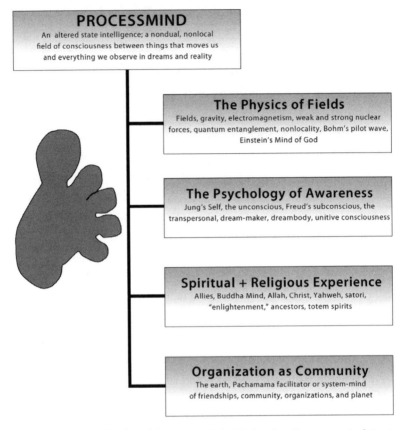

Figure A.1. Unified Fields: Five TOEs Make the Processmind Foot.

Processmind awareness as expressed in physics, psychology, and spirituality alike has three basic levels of awareness: *nonlocality* (an essence-level experience), *bilocality* (the way dream figures and dream-like realities seemingly connect without known causal signal exchanges), and *space-time locality* (consensus reality). These levels correspond to mythic, psychological, and possibly also physical "hyperspaces."

Nonlocality, the deepest level, appears in psychology as presence, the power or feeling that is projected onto or found in earth-based totem field experiences. This is Jung's unconscious, and the alchemist's Unus Mundus. The power of this presence appears again in the quantum waves of physics, in mystical God experiences, and in the "coming together" that sometimes occurs in community life.

Bilocality is my term for the appearance of the processmind in subjective, dualistic, dreamlike experience. Bilocality suggests that two (or more) things are both separate and not separate. We find bilocality in the different local positions of entangled elementary particles, in the diversity and "positions" of dream figures relative to one another, and in our everyday passion for defining, identifying, and entangling things as "good" against "bad," which sometimes switch positions, as if by themselves.

Consensus reality is the real world of here and now, where nothing moves without something communicating with it at speeds no greater than the speed of light. The processmind appears in this world in terms of time, space, and material separation. In personal life we call the state-oriented manifestations of this aspect of the processmind "my" thoughts, "my" body. In physics, consensus reality includes macroscopic objects, space, time, entropy, and elementary particles (though they are analogies of difficult-to-imagine entities). In spiritual traditions, the limitations of consensus reality appear when rules and laws become primary, or when we feel the gods are absent, forgotten, or have died. In consensus reality, "the problem is you over there, not me over here!" Time goes forward, and aging and death are inevitable.

Processmind theories are evolving processes themselves. They require further application and explanation from many sides. We need to know more about how the human community mirrors the entangled physical universe, and how process-oriented ecological awareness can enrich relationships with nature and other human beings. Finally, no theory can ever be considered correct if it does not improve our quality of life, our global situation and international relationships, and our connection to the biosphere. Those improvements are everyone's challenge.

APPENDIX B

PROCESSMIND
COLLAGE PAGES

---

1. Awareness Training (p. 19)

2. Processmind as Body Tendencies (p. 22)

3. The Processmind in Your Body (p. 27)

4. Processmind as Stable Presence (p. 46)

5. The Processmind Field around You (p. 57)

6A. Your Signature Field (p. 71)

6B. Moods and Vector Walking (p. 74)

7A. The Ground of Being around Us (p. 86)

7B. Vector Work in Relationships (p. 89)

8. Kensho in Teamwork (p. 104)

9. Conflict, Death, and Your World Task (p. 114)

10. The City's Processmind (p. 124)

11. Public Stress (p. 134)

12A. Processmind as the Whole Story (p. 150)

12B. Your Belief Processes (p. 155)

13. Finding Your Own Ethics (p. 165)

14. The Unified Field Theory in Life (p. 179)

15. Entangled Flirts (p. 195)

16. The Quantum Entanglement Theater (p. 209)

17. The Facilitator's Power Dance (p. 224)

NOTES

CHAPTER 1. PROCESSMIND AS A FORCE FIELD IN EVERYDAY LIFE AND NEAR DEATH

1. Letter from Einstein to Max Born December 4, 1926 in Albert Einstein, Hedwig und Max Born: *Briefwechsel 1916–1955* (Munich: Nymphenburger Verlagshandlung, 1969).
2. Paul Davies, *The Mind of God: The Scientific Basis for a Rational World* (New York: Touchstone, 1992).
3. After Sara Halprin's death, on the Process Work Institute of Portland's website, www.processwork.org, I found her autobiography and was shocked by some of her words and phrases, which I have italicized. I did not see this autobiography before I had finished writing chapter 1.

I was born in a room *overlooking the Hudson River*, in a hospital in the New York City borough of the Bronx. *All my life I have been attracted to the glint of light on water, and I have felt most at home when I can see a body of water, ocean, lake, or river, but especially river. The river flows downstream and I see a heron standing in the shallows*, motionless, its slender body silhouetted like an Egyptian relief.

Something in me is motionless, like the heron, watching the water and events in the world around me flow past, until a fish, or an opportunity, flashes silver under the surface, and I dive for it.

For many years, books and schools offered opportunity for me to transcend the limitations of my life and I happily followed the river of learning until I became a tenured faculty member at the University of Toronto. Then came a bend in the river—women's studies and filmmaking held me enthralled, and I loved the collaborations that opened to me in both areas. My son was born and watched the lights and shadows on our home movie screen as I nursed him. . . . Before my first book, *Look At My Ugly Face! Myths and Musings on Beauty and Other Perilous Aspects of Women's Appearance* . . . was published, [I dreamed] that *I saw a woman, neither old nor young, sitting in a cave, watching the river flow past. . . .* These days I am privileged to live and work in the home I share with Herb Long, overlooking the Willamette River in the city of Portland, Oregon.

4. Shunryu Suzuki, *Zen Mind, Beginner's Mind*, 34th ed. (New York: Weatherhill, 1995), 84.

Chapter 2. Fields, Lightning, and Enlightenment

1. These known force fields of physics are metaphors: they have local, immediate effects upon objects they touch. The processmind experience may also have such local effects, but in addition it has nonlocal effects that I discuss later in this book.
2. Benjamin Libet, Anthony Freeman, and Keith Sutherland, eds., *The Volitional Brain: Towards a Neuroscience of Free Will* (Exeter: Imprint Academic, 1999), 47–57.
3. "Dreambody" refers to our proprioceptive body experiences, such as aches and pains, which are reflected in dreams. See my book *Dreambody* for more on this subject.

Chapter 3. Zen Metaskills

1. C. G. Jung, "Synchronicity, an Acausal Connecting Principle," in vol. 8 of *Collected Works of C. G. Jung*, edited by Sir Herbert Read, Michael Fordham, and Gerhard Adler, translated by R. F. C. Hull (Princeton: Princeton University Press, 1953).

2. See Amy Mindell, *Metaskills: The Spiritual Art of Therapy* (Tempe, AZ: New Falcon Press, 1995). Sold also by Lao Tse Press, Portland, OR.

3. I use the word *vector* to mean a direction and a magnitude, that is, a feeling of magnitude, that makes us move in a certain direction for any distance. *Vector* is also used as a verb in aviation, meaning "to guide." The word *vector* comes from the Latin *vehere*, which means "to carry," according to Webster's dictionary. The sum of two vectors is the diagonal of a parallelogram. In the case of a right triangle, the sum of the perpendicular lines is the hypotenuse.

4. Takuan Soho, *Unfettered Mind,* translated by William Scott Wilson (Tokyo: Kodansha International, 1986), 47.

5. Ibid (emphasis added).

6. See "Mushin," http://en.wikipedia.org/wiki/Mushin, Oct. 8, 2008.

Chapter 4. The Power of Your Presence

1. Inayat Khan's story of the Little Fish in Paul Reps and Nyogen Senzaki, comp., *Zen Flesh, Zen Bones: A Collection of Zen and Pre-Zen Writings* (North Clarendon, VT: Tuttle Publishing, 1998), 211.

2. L. Kostro, "Einstein and the Ether," *Electronics & Wireless World 94* (1998): 238–39.

3. See my *Quantum Mind and Healing* (Charlottsville, VA: Hampton Roads Publishing, 2004), 227.

4. W. H. Stanner, "After the Dreaming," The Boyer Lectures (ABC radio, Australian Broadcasting Commission, 1968), 44.

5. John (Fire) Lame Deer, and Richard Erdoes, *Lame Deer, Seeker of Visions* (New York: Simon & Schuster, 1972), 197. Thank you to Robert King of Portland, Oregon for this information.

Chapter 5. Your Processmind, the Tao, and Baby Talk

1. In mathematics, the *complex numbers* extend real numbers by adjoining an *imaginary unit*, denoted *i*, which when squared is defined as -1. Complex numbers have the form $a + bi$, where a and b are real numbers called the *real part* and the *imaginary part* of the complex number, respectively.
2. Richard Wilhelm, trans., *The I Ching* or *Book of Changes*, English translation by Cary F. Baynes (Princeton: Princeton University Press, 1990).

Chapter 6. How Your Signature Field Masters Problems

1. F. Collins, M. Guyer, and A. Chakravarti, "Variations on a Theme: Human DNA Sequence Variation," *Science 278* (1997): 1580–81.
2. http://en.wikipedia.org/wiki/Buddha_nature.
3. Thanks to Judy Chambers of Portland, Oregon, for reminding me of Buddha's hand touching the ground.

Chapter 7. The Ground of Being and Satori in Relationships

1. Harris, Ishwar C., *The Laughing Buddha of Tofukuji: The Life of Zen Master Keido Fukushima* (Bloomington, IN: World Wisdom, 2004).

2. Quantum entanglement occurs when the quantum properties of two or more objects must be described in relationship to the other. The state of one is always connected to the state of the other—even though the individual objects may be widely separated in space and time. For example, quantum mechanics holds that the spin of a particle is indeterminate until some physical intervention is made to measure that spin. The spin at that moment is equally likely to be up as to be down. But once the spin of one is measured, the spin of the second particle is known.

3. Rumi is quoted here from Molly Salans, *Storytelling with Children in Crisis* (London: Jessica Kingsley, 2004), 223. This quote is found also in many places on the World Wide Web.

Chapter 9. World War, Death, and World Tasks

1. As of 2009, existing conflicts included: Algeria insurgency 1992 to the present; Angola–Cabinda 1975 to the present; Burma insurgency 1950 to the present; China Senkaku Islands 1968 to the present; China Spratly Islands 1988 to the present; Colombia insurgencies 1970s to the present; Congo (Zaire) War 1998 to the present; Georgia Civil War 1991 to the present; India Assam 1985 to the present; India–Kashmir 1970s to the present; India Naxalite Uprising 1967 to the present; Indonesia Aceh 1986 to the present; Indonesia Kalimantan 1983 to the present; Indonesia Maluku 1999 to the present; Indonesia Papua / West Irian 1963 to the present; Israel–Al-Aqsa Intifada 2000 to the present; Israel–Lebanon 2006 to the present; Ivory Coast Civil War 2002 to the present; Korean War 1953 to the present; Laos Hmong insurgency 2000 to the present; Moldova Transdniester 1991 to the present; Namibia Caprivi Strip 1966 to the present; Nepal Maoists 1996 to the present; Nigeria civil disturbances 1997 to the present; Pakistan–Baluchistan 2004 to the present; Palestine civil war 2007 to the present; Peru Shining Path 1970s to the present; Philippines

Moro uprising 1970s to the present; Russia–Chechen uprising 1992 to the present; Somalia civil war 1991 to the present; Spain–Basque uprising 1970s to the present; Sri Lanka Tamil Separatists 1983 to the present; Sudan–Darfur 1983 to the present; Thailand–Islamic Rebels 2001 to the present; Turkey–Kurdistan 1984 to the present; Uganda civil conflict 1980 to the present; United States–Afghanistan 1980 to the present; United States–Djibouti 2001 to the present; United States–Iraq 1990 to the present; United States–Philippines 1898 to the present; Uzbekistan civil disturbances 2005 to the present; Yemen–Sheik al-Houti 2004 to the present. From http://www.globalsecurity.org/military/world/war/map.htm.

2. See *Quantum Mind*, 503.
3. See *Shaman's Body*, especially the chapter "The Ally's Secret."
4. See *Coma: Key to Awakening*, where I show how awareness ameliorated "Peter's" last moments of life.

CHAPTER 10. THE CITY'S PROCESSMIND: NEW ORLEANS

1. From the PBS (Public Broadcasting Station) transcript of a radio show about New Orleans: http://www.pbs.org/wgbh/amex/neworleans/filmmore/pt.html.
2. See article in the "Adelaide Grid" at http://www.adelaidegrid.warp0.com/.
3. See http://en.wikipedia.org/wiki/Mahalaxmi_Temple_(Mumbai).
4. See http://en.wikipedia.org/wiki/Hoodoo_(folk_magic).

CHAPTER 11. THE WORLD IN YOUR BODY AND YOUR BODY IN THE WORLD

1. I honor the Native American rainbow medicines, though their "rainbow" is different. See Wolf Moondance, *Rainbow Medicine:*

A Visionary Guide to Native American Shamanism (New York: Sterling, 1994).

2. For example, temperature differences in a room cause heat to flow in one direction or another. Likewise, if you open a window, pressure differences make the air flow. "These two flows can be independent or coupled (i.e., one influences the other). Likewise, in the thermoelectric effect, heat can make electricity flow, and electricity can make heat flow." See "Reciprocal Relations in Irreversible Processes," I, *Physics Review 37* (1931): 405–26.

3. Homeostasis is the ability of living beings to regulate a stable, constant internal environment through many small internal adjustments. Claude Bernard, considered the father of modern physiology, published this term for the first time in 1865. The term comes from the Greek *homoios* (same, like, resembling) and *stasis* (to stand).

4. Thanks to Dr. Pierre Morin of Portland, Oregon for introducing me to stress concepts in medicine and to the new idea of "allostasis."

5. The symmetry of nonequilibrium coupled processes in physics is based upon the concept of time reversibility in the quantum world. Lars Onsager received the Nobel prize in physics in 1968 for his 1931 work on reciprocal coupled flows and forces in thermodynamic systems.

Chapter 12. Science, Religion, and God Experience

1. See Paul Davies, *The Mind of God: The Scientific Basis for a Rational World* (New York: Simon & Schuster, 1992).

2. See my books *Sitting in the Fire* and *The Deep Democracy of Open Forums*.

3. A religious survey in the United States showed that 70 percent of all believers in all faiths agreed with the statement, "Many faiths can lead to salvation." Bob Abernathy, *Religion and Ethics*, PBS, June 29, 2009.

4. From Fox News, August 4, 2007, http://www.foxnews.com/story/ 0,2933,294395,00.html.

CHAPTER 13. YOUR (EARTH-BASED) ETHICS

1. The zero-point field is the lowest energy state or ground state of a field in quantum field theory. See John Gribbon, *Q Is for Quantum—An Encyclopedia of Particle Physics* (New York: Touchstone Books, 1998).
2. See my *Quantum Mind*, chapter 17 for more about flirts and their connection to John Cramer's "transactional approach" to quantum theory.
3. "Physics gives rise to observer–participant, observer–participant gives rise to information, information gives rise to physics." J. Wheeler, "Information, Physics, Quantum: The Search for Links," in *Proceedings of the 3rd International Symposium on the Foundation of Quantum Mechanics* (Tokyo: Addison-Wesley, 1989), 354.
4. Christian process theology, suggested by Alfred North Whitehead and written about by John Cobb, agrees that the divine is changed by the believer. See Cobb's *The Process Perspective: Frequently Asked Questions about Process Theology* (Atlanta, GA: Chalice Press, 2003).
5. See my *Shaman's Body*, chapter 14.

CHAPTER 14. MYSTICISM AND UNIFIED FIELDS

1. See my *Sitting in the Fire*, 87.
2. John Ellis seems to have developed the term "TOE" in 1982. See John Ellis, "The Superstring: Theory of Everything, or of Nothing?" *Nature* 323 (1986): 595–98.
3. A good general introduction to space-time is at http://en.wikipedia. org/wiki/Space_time.
4. See appendix A for details about the unified field theory and TOEs.
5. See *Earth-Based Psychology*, 156.

CHAPTER 15. ENTANGLEMENT IN RELIGION, PHYSICS, AND PSYCHOLOGY

1. See these characteristics described in detail, for example, in Wikipedia: http://en.wikipedia.org/wiki/God.
2. See Einstein's article entitled "Can Quantum-Mechanical Description of Physical Reality Be Considered Complete?" *Physical Review* 47 (1935): 777–80. His coauthors were Boris Podolsky and Nathan Rosen.
3. Amit Goswami, *The Self-Aware Universe: How Consciousness Creates the Material World* (New York: Tarcher/Putnam Books, 1993).

CHAPTER 16. ENTANGLEMENT AS A SOFTSKILL IN RELATIONSHIPS

1. I have not been able to identify the source of the term "softskill." It is widely used in business. See: http://en.wikipedia.org/wiki/Soft_skills, October 2009. In contrast to IQ, softskills are often identified with emotional intelligence. Softskills may include negotiation techniques, teamwork ability, or positive attitudes towards serving others. While these softskills are important, for me, "softskill" refers to flowing with the processmind between entangled signals and accusations.

CHAPTER 17. THE WORLD AS A CO-CREATIVE ORGANIZATION

1. See the *San Francisco Chronicle*'s article about this remarkable event at http://www.aamindell.net/download/research/sfchronicle.pdf.
2. Howard Thurman, *Disciplines of the Spirit*, repr. ed. (Richmond, IN: Friends United Press, 2003), 16. See also his "Search for Common

Ground." I am thankful to Dr. John Johnson for introducing me to the work of Howard Thurman.

3. http://en.wikipedia.org/wiki/Howard_Thurman.

4. I am planning a future book on process-oriented ecology and the second training.

CONCLUSION: *UBUNTU*, THE WORLD'S FUTURE

1. "Letter to Max Born," December 4, 1926, in *The Born–Einstein Letters*, translated by Irene Born (New York: Walker, 1971).

2. http://commons.wikimedia.org/wiki/Image:Experience_ubuntu.ogg.

3. http://en.wiktionary.org/wiki/ubuntu#Etymology.

4. http://en.wikipedia.org/wiki/Ahimsa October, 2009.

5. The lyrics of "We Shall Overcome," a protest song that became an anthem of the US civil rights movement, are from a gospel song by Rev. Charles Tindley, an African-American minster from Philadelphia. See http://en.wikipedia.org/wiki/We_Shall_Overcome.

GLOSSARY

big U. The vector describing the overall tendency of an entire world, a group, an individual, or even a particle. The big U is a psychological experience (derived from vector formulations of the quantum wave) related to David Bohm's piloting-guiding function of the system's mind (or more exactly, its **quantum mind**). It is moved by the invisible field of the **processmind.**

bilocality. The two-in-oneness experience of being in two states of mind or two separate locations interconnected through the psychological (i.e., subjective) experience of **nonlocality.**

co-creation. The fieldlike experience of the processmind emerges into a sense of two or more entangled parts. When the everyday mind still has access to the processmind, you can witness and experience the natural flow between parts co-creating new realities. Conscious co-creation creates the **quantum theater.**

compassion. Gaining access to the big U and/or the processmind, being open to all directions and sides; *compass-ion*, meaning a 360-degree "compass" openness and interest in all vectors.

consensus making. The facilitator can help gain agreement by discovering what direction the group would like to take first and by knowing that all of the issues and feelings are important and need to be discussed at some point. Whatever theme is chosen, it is a large umbrella topic with many subthemes, some of which may include other topics mentioned by the group during filtering, that is, the process of sorting for issues.

consensus reality. The generally agreed-upon idea of what is "real." In the twenty-first century, this means that which can be observed "objectively" in time, space, matter, and energy. In today's consensus reality, something moves only if something near it touches or pushes it.

deep democracy. A concept, as well as an elder's multidimensional feeling attitude toward life, that recognizes the basically equal importance of representing **consensus reality** concerns (facts, issues, problems, people), dreamland figures (**roles**, **ghosts**, directions), and the **essence** (common ground) that connects everyone.

double signals. "Second messages" we send of which we are not aware. You can see double signals in dreams and in body postures. For example, I might say verbally that I want to relate to you. That is my intention. However, at the same time I am looking down and not at you. A double signal is usually entangled with what is intended in communication.

dreambody. Body experiences such as a sharp pain mirrored in dreams by symbols such as a knife.

dreamland. A general level of awareness including dreams, dreaming while awake, and nonconsensual experiences (relative to a given community).

edge. A moment when someone speaks but is unable to complete what she or he is saying due to personal reasons or because of actual or perceived group restrictions.

eldership. A universal **metaskill** emerging from your deepest self: your **processmind** and its direction. This skill manifests as a **deeply democratic** attitude that interweaves the equal importance of individual viewpoints, the world as your child, and the grand mystery behind it all.

enlightenment. Processmind awareness that is present most of the time even as you identify with people, your normal identity, time, and space.

entanglement (in physics). Quantum entanglement is a property of a quantum system of two or more objects in which the states of the objects are correlated or linked so that one object can no longer be described without full mention of its counterpart regardless of how close or far they are from one another. This interconnection leads to nonclassical links between remote objects, often referred to as **nonlocality.**

entanglement (in psychology). A metaphor borrowed from quantum physics, meaning an individual or group experience in which parts of emotional systems are connected not only through known causal connections but also through nonlocal means, as if there were no separations between the parts.

essence. The nondual level of awareness, such as "the Tao that can't be said." This level corresponds to experiences which are implicit or not yet explicit to our everyday minds. This is the basic level of the **processmind**, a noncognitive "knowing" that is difficult to explicate.

first and second trainings. In the first training you develop the skills needed for a profession and become aware of your experience as a fact and a **role**, as well as other **ghost roles** and **vectors**. In the second training, you learn to shape-shift at least briefly into the **processmind** and facilitate the relationship between parts of systems. In other words, you are half in the realm of dreaming while half out in reality, facilitating the flow between experiences.

flirts. Flickering, split-second **signals** trying to catch your attention. A flower, for example, may "flirt" with you (and vice versa!). The flirt happens so quickly that we usually pass it by or forget it. Yet in communicating, the flirt plays an important role as a predecessor to signals.

framing. The facilitator can frame, or organize, a discussion by remarking about the different **levels**, or dimensions, about which people are speaking. For example, one person may speak about issues and outer actions (**consensus reality**) while someone else is speaking about feelings (**dreamland**). Then someone else might speak about a common ground (**essence**) that unites the group. The presence of multiple levels can be the source of conflict in itself! The facilitator can frame what is occurring by saying/asking which direction the person or group wishes to focus on first, while acknowledging that the other levels need to be focused on as well.

ghost roles. Part of **dreamland**, these refer to those things that are spoken about but not directly represented by anyone in a given group. Some typical ghosts are ancestors who are spoken about but who are no longer present, the "bad" person who is not in the room, the environment, the president, etc. Getting into, representing, and expressing the views and thoughts of ghosts can be important keys to processes. And it is important to know that everyone shares these ghost roles.

levels. Dimensions of awareness. In this book I focus on three main levels: **consensus reality**, **dreamland**, and the **essence**. *See also* **framing**.

loveland. Your favorite and most consistent earth-based association to the deepest part of you. I also call this earth spot your **processmind**.

metaskill. Defined by Amy in her book *Metaskills* as the overarching quality or feeling behind the use of a skill. The way you say something or do something is a metaskill that can be harsh, helpful, compassionate, playful, scientific, etc.

mythostasis. Includes homeostasis and allostasis (our bodies' abilities to return to normal range of temperature, pressure, and other variables needed for good health) as well as near-death experiences wherein homeostasis and allostasis fail. What seems *not* to fail is our consistent tendency to follow a particular track, as perceived, for instance, in visions and dreams.

nonlocality. In physics, nonlocality is the direct influence of one object on another, distant object, in violation of the principle of locality, which says that an object is influenced only by its immediate surroundings. In psychology, nonlocality is a experience of closeness or interconnection beyond the parameters of time or space. This is usually an altered state / **processmind** experience and quality in which there is no perceived separation between (entangled) particles, parts, **flirts**, etc.

open forum. A structured, deeply democratic meeting, person-to-person or in cyberspace, in which everyone feels represented and social issues as well as the deepest feelings and dreams of the participants are included. The open forum method emphasizes the more linear style of the generally nonlinear worldwork approach in which the facilitator slows down events as needed and intervenes more often.

participant-facilitator. In processwork, the concept of leader and facilitator is understood as a shared and nonlocal role. The traditional concept of participant has changed; participants or citizens are called "participant-facilitators" (just as the leader-facilitator is now termed the leader-follower).

processmind. The deepest part of ourselves, associated with a part of our body and the power of an earth location. Just as the earth underlies all forms of human and natural events in the biosphere, the processmind is the dreaming intelligence and field that organizes all our experiences; hence it is a key dimension all facilitators need to access. The processmind is a nonlocal "oneness" experience and appears in dreams and reality as the diversity of things catching our attention and interest.

process-oriented ecology. Studies our "home", i.e., the earth and its interactional processes including but not limited to plants, animals (including people), real and dreamlike objects and energies. Based on deep democracy, "p.o.e." is transdisciplinary, including at minimum the physical, biological, and psychological sciences as well as mythic understandings of the world.

quantum mind. The processmind's conceptual predecessor in my work, reflected in the math and laws of quantum physics. As seen in the math of physics, the quantum mind shows the tendency to self-reflect, to produce and notice quick, easily marginalized **flirts** catching our attention, and to collapse or repress the wave functions or dreams to create reality. See appendix A for more.

quantum theater (or quantum entanglement theater). A process experience that creates and facilitates the entanglement between dreamlike pairs of opposites. This theater, unlike other kinds of role awareness and role play, is based upon noncognitive, essence-like experiences of the processmind.

quantum wave function. A mathematical equation used in quantum theory to describe physical systems. The wave function describes the "state space," the complex number "map" of all possible states of the system. The laws of quantum mechanics, represented in part by Schrödinger's equation, describe how the wave function evolves over time. The values of the wave function are complex numbers— the squares whose absolute values indicate the probability that the system will be in any of the possible states.

relationship work. As suggested in this book, relationship work implies finding the **processmind** or land, between and encompassing two or more people, and from that viewpoint noticing the edges and signals, and facilitating the flirts, dreams, signals, and feelings that arise. Then use the quantum theater as needed.

role. Part of the **dreamland** aspect of group process. Although each role (e.g., boss, underling, patient, helper) seems located within a given individual or group, it is actually an evolving time-spirit, a nonlocal transforming spirit of the times that needs everyone to fill it. In other words, each role is much greater than any one individual or group. And each of us is bigger than any one role. Roles are entangled.

role switching. There is a natural tendency to role switch. That is, we find that we may identify with a particular role but then at a given point notice that we feel pulled to represent another role, or that we *are* in another role. For example, someone in a social-service organization who is identified as a helper of others who are suffering and in need of care may begin to speak about her or his own suffering. At that moment, she or he has switched into the role of the "others" who need care. Noticing and allowing yourself to switch roles, sensing when you are in one role and when you begin to move to another, is an awareness practice. To do this best, find the **processmind** of the situation and tangle-dance, as described in the last chapter.

second training. *See* **first and second trainings.**

signal. Signals may originate as almost imperceptible experiences that only the observer notices. Otherwise, signals are perceived pieces of information, communicated by words, sounds, actions, gestures, or body feelings. Signals have a local appearance, but may be nonlocally entangled with communication partners at a distance.

softskill. The method of using the processmind fluidly to understand roles and switch. The ineffable guidance from mythic, earth-based sources and the processmind that can feel into and role play all sides of a situation. Contrasts with more conventional skills that involve prelearned methods and programs. At present, the processmind softskill is perhaps the most useful method to facilitate all kinds of situations and make everyone feel understood.

superposition. The sum of all experiences around a given observation, or the vector sum of all directions representing these experiences.

tangle-dance. Based on the concept of entanglement in physics and its psychological counterpart, parts are seen as symmetrically and dynamically (thus the dance element) interconnected. For example, if A says, "Because you did this, I did that," B might typically respond, "No! The opposite! Because *you* did this, I did that!" But when using the tangle-dance approach, the observer then relaxes, identifies with the processmind, and allows it to "tangle" between A and B until they co-create new solutions.

teamwork. If a team is a group of individuals joined together for a common task, then teamwork occurs when the team is aware of its mission and uses its processmind.

totem spirit. In Aboriginal cultures around the world, a totem is an entity believed to watch over or assist a group of people, be it a family, clan, or tribe. This spirit is often a symbol of the processmind.

ubuntu. The central and southern African community ethic that stresses the interconnectedness between all peoples, as in the phrase, "I am because you are."

vector. A mathematical term for an arrow indicating, for example, direction or velocity. I use vectors to symbolize our subjective or dreamlike sense of earth-based direction. The earth pulls or moves us in certain directions at different times. When we walk and follow the direction or vector of an experience, we sense some energy, power, and rhythm as well as the path's meaning.

world work. A small- and large-group method that uses deep democracy to address the issues of groups and organizations of all kinds. World work employs the power of an organization's or city's dreamlike background (e.g., projections, gossip, roles, and creative fantasy). World work facilitators listen to the land, do innerwork, and practice outer communication skills involving role consciousness and signal and rank awareness to enrich organizational life. World work has been successfully used in work with multicultural, multileveled communities; universities; small and large international organizations; city hot spots; political situations; and world conflict zones.

Zen mind. A Zen Buddhist concept. In *Zen Mind, Beginner's Mind*, Shunryu Suzuki Roshi says: "The world is its own magic. . . . Zen mind is one of those enigmatic phrases used by Zen teachers to throw you back upon yourself, to make you go behind the words themselves and begin wondering . . . do I really know what my own mind is? . . . And if you should then try to sit physically still for a while to see if you can discover just what your mind is, to see if you can locate it—then you have begun the practice of Zen, then you have begun to realize the unrestricted mind." Zen mind seems to be a processmind-like concept.

BIBLIOGRAPHY

Cheshire, Stuart. "Collected Quotes from Albert Einstein." Retrieved December 6, 2004, from http://rescomp.stanford.edu/~cheshire/EinsteinQuotes.html.

Chodron, Pema. *Practicing Peace in Times of War*. Boston: Shambhala, 2006.

Cobbs, John. *The Process Perspective: Frequently Asked Questions about Process Theology*. Atlanta, GA: Chalice Press, 2003.

Collins, F., M. Guyer, and A. Chakravarti. "Variations on a Theme: Human DNA Sequence Variation." *Science* 278 (1997): 1580–81.

Cramer, John G. "An Overview of the Transactional Interpretation of Quantum Mechanics." *International Journal of Theoretical Physics* 27, no. 2 (1988): 227–36.

Davies, Paul. *The Mind of God: The Scientific Basis for a Rational World*. New York: Simon & Schuster, 1992.

Einstein, Albert. *Cosmic Religion: With Other Opinions and Aphorisms*. New York: Covici-Friede, 1931. Reprinted 2007.

———. "Letter to Max Born," December 4, 1926, in *The Born-Einstein Letters*. Edited by Max Born. New York: Walker & Co, 1926. Reprinted 1971.

Ellis, John. "The Superstring: Theory of Everything, or of Nothing?" *Nature* 323 (1986): 595–98.

Goswami, Amit, Richard E. Reed, and Maggie Goswami. *The Self-Aware Universe: How Consciousness Creates the Material World*. New York: Tarcher/Putnam, 1993.

Gribbon, John. Q Is for Quantum: An Encyclopedia of Particle Physics. New York: Touchstone Books, 1998.

Harris, Ishwar C. *The Laughing Buddha of Tofukuji: The Life of Zen Master Keido Fukushima*. Bloomington, IN: World Wisdom, 2004.

I Ching or Book of Changes. Translated into German by Richard Wilhelm, English translation by Cary F. Baynes. Princeton: Princeton University Press, 1990.

Lame Deer, John (Fire), and Richard Erdoes. *Lame Deer, Seeker of Visions*. New York: Simon & Schuster, 1972.

Mindell, Amy. *Metaskills: The Spiritual Art of Therapy*. Tempe, AZ: New Falcon Press, 1995.

———. "World Work and the Politics of Dreaming, or Why Dreaming Is Crucial for World Process." http://www.aamindell.net/blog/ww-themes, November, 2007.

Mindell, Arnold. *Coma, Key to Awakening: The Dreambody near Death*. Boulder, CO: Shambhala, 1989. Reprinted by Lao Tse Press (Portland, OR), 2010.

———. *The Deep Democracy of Open Forums: How to Transform Organizations into Communities*. Charlottesville, VA: Hampton Roads, 2002.

———. *Dreambody: The Body's Role in Revealing the Self*. Boston, MA: Sigo Press, 1982. Reprinted by Viking-Penguin-Arkana (London & New York), 1986; by Lao Tse Press (Portland, OR), 2000.

———. *The Dreambody in Relationships*. London & New York: Viking-Penguin-Arkana, 1987. Reprinted by Lao Tse Press (Portland, OR), 2000.

———. *Dreaming While Awake: Techniques for 24-Hour Lucid Dreaming*. Charlottesville, VA: Hampton Roads, 2000.

———. *Earth-Based Psychology: Path Awareness from the Teachings of Don Juan, Richard Feynman, and Lao Tse*. Portland, OR: Lao Tse Press, 2007.

———. *The Leader as Martial Artist: An Introduction to Deep Democracy.* San Francisco: Harper Collins, 1992.

———. *Quantum Mind: The Edge between Physics and Psychology.* Portland, OR: Lao Tse Press, 2000.

———. *The Quantum Mind and Healing: How to Listen and Respond to Your Body's Symptoms.* Charlottesville, VA: Hampton Roads, 2004.

———. *The Shaman's Body: A New Shamanism for Health, Relationships, and Community.* San Francisco: Harper Collins, 1993.

———. *Sitting in the Fire: Large Group Transformation through Diversity and Conflict.* Portland, OR: Lao Tse Press, 1995.

———. *The Year One: Global Process Work.* London & New York: Viking-Penguin-Arkana, 1989.

Moondance, Wolfe. *Rainbow Medicine: A Visionary Guide to Native American Shamanism.* New York: Sterling Publishing, 1994.

Onsager, Lars. "Reciprocal Relations in Irreversible Processes," *Physics Review* 37 (1931): 405–26.

Simon, Ronald, T., and Marc Estrin. *Rehearsing with the Gods: Photographs and Essays on the Bread and Puppet Theater.* White River Junction, VT: Chelsea Green Publishing, 2004.

Suzuki, Shunryu. *Zen Mind, Beginner's Mind.* 34th ed. New York: Weatherhill, 1995.

Thurman, Howard. *Disciplines of the Spirit.* Reprint. Richmond, IN: Friends United Press, 2003.

———. *The Search for Common Ground.* New York: Harper & Row, 1973.

Wheeler, John. "Information, Physics, Quantum: The Search for Links." Proceedings of the 3rd International Symposium on the Foundation of Quantum Mechanics, Tokyo, 1989.

Wolf, Fred Alan. *The Dreaming Universe: A Mind-Expanding Journey into the Realm Where Psyche and Physics Meet.* New York: Touchstone, 1995.

———. *Star Wave: Mind, Consciousness, and Quantum Physics.* New York: Macmillan, 1984.

ILLUSTRATION CREDITS

Figure 0.1. *Wikimedia*, image "Albert Einstein in Later Years," http://commons.wikimedia.org/wiki/File:Albert_Einstein_in_later_years.jpg (accessed October 10, 2009).

CHAPTER 1

Figure 1.1. Photo of Sara Halprin by Herb Long. "Silhouette of Man Fishing at Sunset" image file at http://www.istockphoto.com/file_closeup.php?id=4625443. "Portland Skyline" image file at http://www.istockphoto.com/stock-photo-8773692-portland-skyline.php. *Wikipedia*, image "Mallard," http://en.wikipedia.org/wiki/File:Male_mallard3.jpg. (accessed October 13, 2009).

CHAPTER 3

Figure 3.3. Schrödinger's Cat. *Wikipedia*, image "Schrödinger's cat," http://en.wikipedia.org/wiki/Wikipedia:Featured_picture_candidates/Schr%C3%B6dinger%27s_cat (accessed October 12, 2009).

CHAPTER 4

Figure 4.1. "Tropical fish French Angelfish" image file at http://www.istockphoto.com/stock-photo-9950680-tropical-fish-french-angelfish.php.

Figure 4.2. "Relaxing on Remote Beach," image file at http://www. istockphoto.com/stock-photo-4701539-relaxing-on-remote-beach.php (accessed October 13, 2009). "Fairy Forest" image file at http://www. istockphoto.com/file_closeup.php?id=2192531 (accessed October 13, 2009).

Figure 4.4. "Messy Room" image file at http://www.istockphoto.com/ stock-illustration-4429733-messy-room.php (accessed October 10, 2009).

CHAPTER 5

Figure 5.4. "Magnetic Field of the Earth" image file at http://hyperphysics. phy-astr.gsu.edu/hbase/magnetic/magearth.html (accessed June 10, 2009). Thanks to Rod Nave and NASA for Rod's educational "hyper physics" work.

Figure 5.6. "Synaesthesia." Thanks to Andrew Done for a similar sketch on Wikipedia, image "Booba-Kiki," http://en.wikipedia.org/wiki/ Synesthesia (accessed June 10, 2008).

CHAPTER 6

Figure 6.2. Fantova Collection of Albert Einstein, Manuscripts Division, Department of Rare Books and Special Collections, Princeton University Library. Princeton, New Jersey.

Figure 6.3. "The Buddha Touching the Earth" image found at http:// pranayogastudio.com/. Thanks to Anna Siudy.

CHAPTER 8

Figure 8.2. "Garden spirit stick" image thanks to http://www. gardenspiritsticks.com/gallery.shtml (accessed October 13, 2009). Wikipedia image "Melsquir" http://en.wikipedia.org/wiki/File:Melsquir. jpg (accessed October 13, 2009). Photo of Amy by Nader Shabahangi.

Figure 8.3. Wikimedia, image "Totem haida," http://commons.wikimedia. org/wiki/File:Totem_haida.jpg (accessed October 10, 2009).

Figure 8.4. *Fishing for Souls*, Adriaen Pietersz van de Venne, 1614, Rijksmuseum, Amsterdam.

Figure 8.6. Statue of Liberty "Freedom" image at http://www.istockphoto. com/stock-photo-5487343-freedom.php.

CHAPTER 10

Figure 10.1. Wikipedia, image "Orleans.bourbon," http://en.wikipedia.org/ wiki/File:Orleans.bourbon.arp.750pix.jpg (accessed October 10, 2009).

Figure 10.2. "Katrina Ninth Ward Levees and Homeless" image at http:// www.thewe.cc/weplanet/news/americas/us/katrina_ninth_ward_levees_ and_homeless.htm.

CHAPTER 11

Figure 11.2. "Monterosso Al Mare, Cinque Terre, Italy" image at http:// www.istockphoto.com/stock-photo-3355570-monterosso-al-mare- cinque-terre-italy.php.

CHAPTER 12

Figure 12.1. Wikipedia, image "Flammarion," http://en.wikipedia.org/ wiki/File:Flammarion.jpg (accessed October 10, 2009).

CHAPTER 15

Figure 15.2. "Artist's Concept of Entanglement" NASA image at http://www. jpl.nasa.gov/news/news.cfm?release=2003-047 (accessed June 4, 2009).

CHAPTER 16

Figure 16.5. "Wind Gusts from Hurricane Gustav" image at http://www. istockphoto.com/stock-photo-7101199-wind-gusts-from-hurricane- gustav.php (accessed October 10, 2009).

CHAPTER 17

Figure 17.2. Wikipedia, image "Earth-crust-cutaway-english," http://en.wikipedia.org/wiki/File:Earth-crust-cutaway-english.svg (accessed October 10, 2009).

Figure 17.3. Earth and moon from Galileo probe, NASA, Jan 02 1990, http://www.physics.unlv.edu/~jeffery/astro/earth/nasa_earth_moon_001.jpg (accessed October 12, 2009).

CONCLUSION

Figure C.1. Wikipedia, image "Huli wigman," http://en.wikipedia.org/wiki/File:Huli_wigman.jpg (accessed October 13, 2009).

Figure C.3. *Ubuntu* Batik purchased from the artist Richard Kimbo on a Nairobi street, 1988.

Figure C.4. Wikipedia, image "Jain hand," http://en.wikipedia.org/wiki/File:Jain_hand.svg (accessed October 13, 2009).

INDEX

Related Quest Titles

Earth Energies, by Serge King
Gaia's Hidden Life, compiled by Shirley J. Nicholson,
with Brenda Rosen
Science and the Sacred, by Ravi Ravindra
*Thriving in the Crosscurrent: Clarity and Hope
in a Time of Cultural Sea Change*, by Jim Kenney
*The Visionary Window: A Quantum Physicist's
Guide to Enlightenment* , by Amit Goswami

About the Author

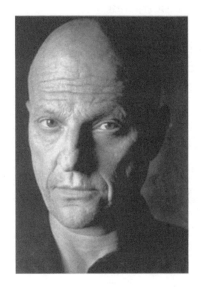

Arnold (Arny) Mindell has a MS from the Massachusetts Institute of Technology and a PhD in psychology, as well as being a Jungian analyst. He is the author of twenty books in twenty-three languages, including *Dreambody*, *The Shaman's Body*, *Quantum Mind*, and *Quantum Mind and Healing*. He is well known in the area of conflict management and for his integration of psychology and physics; his work on dreams, bodywork, and relationships; and his mode of interventions in near-death situations.

In the 1970s, Arny developed process work, or what is called today "process-oriented psychology." In the 1980s, he and his wife, Dr. Amy Mindell, together with their many colleagues, cofounded the original school of process-oriented psychology in Zurich, Switzerland. By the 1990s Arny had expanded process work to include quantum theory and a deeper form of democracy that applied to all states of consciousness for individuals and groups. Now process work is used in individual therapy, body problems, coma and near-death experiences, and large-group and organizational change management. Arny's recent research and practice has also lead to "process-oriented ecology," integrating large-group conflict work with environmental issues. Today, the Mindells consult and work as facilitators on community and conflict problems for groups, cities, and governments worldwide.